Lecture Notes in Computer Science 13226

More information about this series at https://link.springer.com/bookseries/558

Fabrizio Montesi ·
George Angelos Papadopoulos ·
Wolf Zimmermann (Eds.)

Service-Oriented and Cloud Computing

9th IFIP WG 6.12 European Conference, ESOCC 2022
Wittenberg, Germany, March 22–24, 2022
Proceedings

 Springer

Editors
Fabrizio Montesi 🄳
University of Southern Denmark
Odense, Denmark

George Angelos Papadopoulos 🄳
University of Cyprus
Nicosia, Cyprus

Wolf Zimmermann
Martin Luther University Halle-Wittenberg
Halle (Saale), Germany

ISSN 0302-9743   ISSN 1611-3349 (electronic)
Lecture Notes in Computer Science
ISBN 978-3-031-04717-6   ISBN 978-3-031-04718-3 (eBook)
https://doi.org/10.1007/978-3-031-04718-3

This Springer imprint is published by the registered company Springer Nature Switzerland AG
The registered company address is: Gewerbestrasse 11, 6330 Cham, Switzerland

Preface

Service-oriented and cloud computing have made a huge impact both on the software industry and on the research community. Today, service and cloud technologies are applied to build large-scale software landscapes as well as to provide single software services to end users. Services today are independently developed and deployed as well as freely composed while they can be implemented in a variety of technologies, a quite important fact from a business perspective. Similarly, cloud computing aims at enabling flexibility by offering a centralized sharing of resources. The industry's need for agile and flexible software and IT systems has made cloud computing the dominating paradigm for provisioning computational resources in a scalable, on-demand fashion. Nevertheless, service developers, providers, and integrators still need to create methods, tools, and techniques to support cost-effective and secure development as well as the use of dependable devices, platforms, services, and service-oriented applications in the cloud.

The European Conference on Service-Oriented and Cloud Computing (ESOCC) is the premier conference on advances in the state of the art and practice of service-oriented computing and cloud computing in Europe. The main objectives of this conference are to facilitate the exchange between researchers and practitioners in the areas of service-oriented computing and cloud computing, as well as to explore the new trends in those areas and foster future collaborations in Europe and beyond. The 9th edition of ESOCC, ESOCC 2022, was supposed to be held at Lutherstadt Wittenberg, Germany, from March 22 until March 24, 2022. Due to the COVID-19 pandemic situation it was held as a virtual conference.

ESOCC 2022 was a multi-event conference aiming at covering both an academic and an industrial audience. The main event mapped to the main research track which focused on the presentation of cutting-edge research in both the service-oriented and cloud computing areas. In conjunction, an industrial track was also held to bring together academia and industry through showcasing the application of service-oriented and cloud computing research, especially in the form of case studies, in industry. Overall, 17 submissions were received out of which eight outstanding were accepted—six full papers and two short papers.

Each submission was peer-reviewed by three main reviewers, comprising either Program Committee (PC) members or their colleagues. The PC chairs would like to thank all the reviewers that participated in the reviewing process. Their comments were essential for improving the quality of the received manuscripts and especially for giving constructive comments to the authors of papers that, in their current forms, were rejected for ESOCC 2022.

The attendees of ESOCC had the opportunity to follow an outstanding keynote that was part of the conference program. The keynote was conducted by Uwe Assmann, professor and former dean of the Faculty of Computer Science at Dresden University of Technology, Germany. This keynote introduced an exciting application of fog computing: a gas sniffing sensor network for remote operation in dangerous areas.

The additional events held at ESOCC 2022 included the PhD symposium, enabling PhD students to present their work in front of real experts, as well as a projects track, providing researchers with the opportunity to present the main research results that they have achieved in the context of currently operating EU projects and national projects. Further, ESOCC 2022 included the organization of satellite workshops. All these events will be accompanied by respective proceedings which will be published separately.

The PC chairs and the general chair would like to gratefully thank all the people involved in making ESOCC 2022 a success. This includes both the PC members and their colleagues who assisted in the reviews, as well as the organizers of the industry track, the PhD symposium, the projects track, and the workshops. A special applause should also go to Maik Boltze, Mandy Weissbach, and Ramona Vahrenhold for their administrative support and for managing the virtual conference rooms. Finally, a special thanks goes to all the authors of the manuscripts submitted to ESOCC 2022, the presenters of the accepted papers who made interesting and fascinating presentations of their work, and the active attendees of the conference who initiated interesting discussions and gave fruitful feedback to the presenters. All these people have not only enabled the successful organization and execution of ESOCC 2022 but also an active and vibrant community which continuously contributes to the research in service-oriented and cloud computing. This also encourages ESOCC to keep supporting and enlarging its community, by providing a forum in which new research outcomes can be shared and discussions on how to achieve greater impact can be held.

March 2022

Fabrizio Montesi
George A. Papadopoulos
Wolf Zimmermann

Organization

ESOCC 2022 was organized by Martin Luther University Halle-Wittenberg, Germany.

Organizing Committee

General Chair

Wolf Zimmermann   Martin Luther University Halle-Wittenberg, Germany

Program Chairs

Fabrizio Montesi   University of Southern Denmark, Denmark
George A. Papadopoulos   University of Cyprus, Cyprus

Industry Track Chair

Andreas Both   Anhalt University of Applied Sciences, Germany

Workshop Chairs

Guadalupe Ortiz   University of Cadiz, Spain
Christian Zirpins   Karlsruhe University of Applied Sciences, Germany

Projects Track Chair

Damian Tamburri   Eindhoven University of Technology, The Netherlands

Ph.D. Symposium Chairs

Jacopo Soldani   University of Pisa, Italy
Massimo Villari   University of Messina, Italy

Steering Committee

Antonio Brogi   University of Pisa, Italy
Schahram Dustdar   TU Wien, Austria

Paul Grefen	Eindhoven University of Technology, The Netherlands
Einar Broch Johnson	University of Oslo, Norway
Kyriakos Kritikos	ICS-FORTH and University of the Aegean, Greece
Winfried Lamersdorf	University of Hamburg, Germany
Flavio de Paoli	University of Milano-Bicocca, Italy
Cesare Pautasso	University of Lugano, Switzerland
Ernesto Pimentel	University of Malaga, Spain
Pierluigi Plebani	Politecnico di Milano, Italy
Ulf Schreier	Hochschule Furtwangen University, Germany
Stefan Schulte	Technical University of Hamburg-Harburg, Germany
Massimo Villari	University of Messina, Italy
Olaf Zimmermann	University of Applied Sciences Rapperswil, Switzerland
Wolf Zimmermann	Martin Luther University Halle-Wittenberg, Germany

Program Committee

Marco Aiello	University of Groningen, The Netherlands
Vasilios Andrikopoulos	University of Groningen, The Netherlands
Luciano Baresi	Politecnico di Milano, Italy
Marco Comuzzi	Ulsan National Institute of Science and Technology, South Korea
Luca Davoli	University of Parma, Italy
Elisabetta Di Nitto	Politechnico di Milano, Italy
Marios Dikaiakos	University of Cyprus, Cyprus
Schahram Dustdar	TU Wien, Austria
Rik Eshuis	Eindhoven University of Technology, The Netherlands
Ilche Georgievski	University of Stuttgart, Germany
Saverio Giallorenzo	University of Southern Denmark, Denmark
Paul Grefen	Eindhoven University of Technology, The Netherlands
Thomas Gschwind	IBM Zurich Research Lab, Switzerland
Martin Henkel	Stockholm University, Sweden
Kung-Kiu Lau	University of Manchester, UK
Zoltan Adam Mann	University of Duisburg-Essen, Germany
Jacopo Mauro	University of Southern Denmark, Denmark
Claus Pahl	Free University of Bozen-Bolzano, Italy
George Pallis	University of Cyprus, Cyprus

Ernesto Pimentel	University of Malaga, Spain
Dumitru Roman	SINTEF, Norway
Florian Rademacher	Fachhochschule Dortmund, Germany
Ulf Schreier	University of Applied Sciences Furtwangen, Germany
Sabine Sachweh	Fachhochschule Dortmund, Germany
Stefan Schulte	TU Hamburg, Germany
Jacopo Soldani	University of Pisa, Italy
Massimo Villari	University of Messina, Italy
Mandy Weissbach	Martin Luther University Halle-Wittenberg, Germany
Stefan Wesner	University of Ulm, Germany
Robert Woitsch	BOC Asset Management, Germany
Gianluigi Zavattaro	University of Bologna, Italy
Christian Zirpins	University of Applied Sciences Karlsruhe, Germany

Contents

Serverless

Invited Talk

Sniffbots to the Rescue – Fog Services for a Gas-Sniffing Immersive Robot Collective

Uwe Aßmann[1]([✉]) [iD], Mikhail Belov[1], Thanh-Tien Tenh Cong[1],
Waltenegus Dargie[1] [iD], Jianjun Wen[1], Leon Urbas[2], Candy Lohse[2],
Luis Antonio Panes-Ruiz[3] [iD], Leif Riemenschneider[3] [iD], Bergoi Ibarlucea[3] [iD],
Gianaurelio Cuniberti[3] [iD], Mohamad Moner Al Chawa[4] [iD],
Christoph Grossmann[5], Steffen Ihlenfeld[5], Ronald Tetzlaff[4] [iD],
Sergio A. Pertuz[1] [iD], and Diana Goehringer[1] [iD]

[1] Fakultät Informatik, Technische Universität Dresden, Dresden, Germany
{uwe.assmann,mikhail.belov,thanh-tien.tenh_cong,waltenegus.dargie,
jianjun.wen,sergio.pertuz,diana.goehringer}@tu-dresden.de
[2] Fakultät Elektrotechnik und Informationstechnik, Technische Universität Dresden,
Dresden, Germany
leon.urbas@tu-dresden.de
[3] Fakultät für Maschinenwesen, Technische Universität Dresden, Dresden, Germany
{luis_antonio.panes-ruiz,leif.riemenschneider,bergoi.ibarlucea,
gianaurelio.cuniberti}@tu-dresden.de
[4] Institute of Circuits and Systems, Technische Universität Dresden,
Dresden, Germany
{mohamad_moner.al_chawa,ronald.tetzlaff}@tu-dresden.de
[5] Institute of Mechatronic Engineering, Technische Universität Dresden,
Dresden, Germany
steffen.ihlenfeldt@tu-dresden.de
http://sniffbot.inf.tu-dresden.de

Abstract. Gas accidents frequently turn industrial or civil structures into extremely dangerous environments. Disasters like the Ahrtal flood in summer 2021 destroy infrastructures such as the gas grid and the power grid, so that people loose control and suddenly find themselves confronted with explosions, suffocation, and death. This paper presents a case study of a robot collective identifying gas leaks with a gas-sniffing wireless sensor network, while providing immersive inspection and teleoperation in the dangerous areas. So-called SNIFFBOTS work in a minimal communication infrastructure, construct world maps autonomously, use them to find gas leaks, remotely inspect, and attempt to close them. To this end, the fog of a SNIFFBOT should offer services, such as sniff-sensor data aggregation, calculation of points of interest in 2-D and 3-D, virtual reality immersion, remote gripping, as well as autonomous control of flying and driving. While this paper discusses a prototype system still under development, the experiments show the fantastic capabilities of modern gas-sniffing sensors in an immersive robotic fog. SNIFFBOTS, though, at this moment in time, being very expensive robot collectives,

Published by Springer Nature Switzerland AG 2022
F. Montesi et al. (Eds.): ESOCC 2022, LNCS 13226, pp. 3–28, 2022.
https://doi.org/10.1007/978-3-031-04718-3_1

will be a very valuable aid in the future to save the life of people in gas disasters.

Keywords: Cyber physical systems · robotics · UAV · wireless sensor networks · tele-operation · immersion · gas sensors

1   Introduction

Every year several chemical accidents occur around the world, turning inhabitable regions into places dangerous to work and to live in, at least temporarily. Some work environments, such as chemical factories, underground mining, and oil exploration, inherently expose employees to dangerous gases even when there are no conspicuous accidents. Understandably, operating in these environments require stringent safety regulations to prevent detrimental accidents and loss of human lives.

As an example, consider the flood of summer 2021 in the Ahrtal in Germany [44] (Fig. 1). Within several hours, a complete valley of more than 30 km length was flooded and destroyed. Not only houses, bridges and streets were overwhelmed by a ferocious river, but also vital infrastructure was instantly disrupted, including 113 km of gas pipelines and 250 house gas ports, revealing many gas leaks at the same time. This created very dangerous situations: More than 150 people were killed while sleeping, fleeing, or trying to rescue household items or other persons. 17,000 others are still grappling with damaged houses or destroyed properties. The repair of the gas infrastructure took more than 4 months and cost more than 25M€ [37]. Though the German parliament initially approved 30 billion Euros to support the people who are affected by the damage, it has already become clear that the reconstruction of the region will cost much more.

Similarly, in various chemical industries and oil refineries, toxic gases are produced as by-products and transported from one place to another. Some of them, such as Ammonia and Hydrogen Sulphide, belong to the most difficult gases to handle [1]. While leaking gases cause a considerable harm to employees and the environment, damages in pipelines are difficult to locate and to repair due to the considerable length of the pipelines.

Is it possible to monitor disaster areas and large chemical plants alike with the aid of state-of-the-art technology and fix gas pipeline damages as swiftly as possible? Such questions can be answered in the affirmative with the advent of *Immersive Robot Collectives (IRCs)* carrying out several of the required tasks at the same time: inspect the area of interest from remote; localise and estimate the extent of damage; determine rescue paths and entries into facilities; and carry out actual repair operations.

The purpose of this paper is to present the prototype of such a system – a tele-operated, sniffing, multi-robot collective – and report initial results. The SNIFFBOT robot collective, built at the Technische Universität Dresden, provides immersion to orient, monitor, and recognize remote events and situations. It

Fig. 1. Destroyed infrastructure in the Ahrtal, an adequate field for a sniffing IRC (source: https://de.wikipedia.org/wiki/Datei:Hochwasser_in_Altenahr_Altenburg.jpg)

enables remote sniffing of dangerous gases to identify important points of interest in an area, tele-inspection, as well as tele-operated gripping. While SNIFFBOT is certainly not the first robot collective for sniffing dangerous gases, it offers four major innovations: (a) a big artificial nose enabled by a Wireless Sensor Network (WSN), (b) a nano-nose sensing with nano-materials, (c) a 3-D nose by enabling 3-D identification of gas leak positions, (d) and a mobile human avatar for tele-inspection and -manipulation. This paper discusses the problem area, the distributed cloud and fog services that are required for these three innovations, and reports an initial implementation and experimental results.

The remaining part of this paper is organized as follows: In Sect. 2, we unfold the top-level components of the SNIFFBOT IRC. In Sect. 3, we propose a service architecture of a Sniffbot collective and discuss their interactions. In Sect. 4, we present the results of several experiments in the field, in particular about sniffing and immersion. Section 5 compares to related work, and Sect. 6 wraps up.

2   Sniffing Immersive Robot Collectives

In the context of the project *Sniffing Dangerous Gases with Immersive Robots* (SNIFFBOT), we are developing an IRC for remotely discovering and monitoring toxic gases, such as Ammonia (NH_3) and Hydrogen Sulfide (H_2S), both in disaster regions (Fig. 1), as well as industrial complexes, such as oil refineries. The distributed software architecture of SNIFFBOT is organized as a *fog* with four subnetworks. For sniffing the gases, the SNIFFBOT collective uses novel highly-sensitive nanosensors, which are integrated into nodes of a self-organizing WSN to support in-network processing, high spatio-temporal sensing, and multi-hop communication (Fig. 2, left). The network interacts with mobile land robots and drones (henceforth, *mobile agents*), both to minimize human involvement and to extend the communication range of the sensing system (Fig. 2, middle). The mobile agents can be used to connect the WSN with a remote control station, as can be seen in Fig. 5. The WSN regularly sends partially processed data to a fog service on the remote control station, which analyzes the data, generates candidate positions for gas leaks, *Point of Interest* (PoI), and coordinates with mobile agents to localize and navigate to the region of interest. An additional wireless Positioning Network serves for navigation (Fig. 2, right). In the surrounding of a Point of Interest (PoI), i.e., on the *last mile*[1], the robot collective is designed to provide immersive experience for a remote human *immersion operator* who need not enter the monitored region (Fig. 2, lower part). Since all sensor nodes and robots in the fog are operated on batteries, no global communication infrastructure is required.

In a disaster scenario, without any global infrastructure available, the SNIFF-BOT immersive robot collective must master a number of tasks structured into 6 phases:

1. In the first phase, a land robot constructs a 2-D world map of the environment using SLAM algorithms, e.g., 20 m around the center focal point (localization phase).
2. Using the world map, the drones deploy the sensor nodes in the environment (dropping phase).
3. Then, the sensor net attempts to find interesting gas leaks in the area and generates PoI on the world map (PoI identification phase).
4. The land robot navigates to the PoI (navigation phase)
5. and enables a human operator to inspect the surrounding of the PoI (last-mile immersive inspection phase).
6. The operator may use the gripper of the land robot to attempt to close the gas leak (repair phase).

In the second scenario, the regular monitoring of the structural health of pipelines in a chemical industry complex, there is a global infrastructure available, so that localization and navigation tasks are simplified. Moreover, workers can deploy the sensor network permanently, so that the dropping phase can be spared. In both scenarios, the drones can be equipped with sniffing sensors themselves so that they can attempt to discover the gas leak (flying exploration phase [36]).

The following discusses the sub-networks of the SNIFFBOT fog and their relationships in more detail (Fig. 2). All components take over some services for the SNIFFBOT innovations and the overall task, the localization and repair of gas leaks (Sect. 3).

---

[1] Actually, it is the area of the *last meters*.

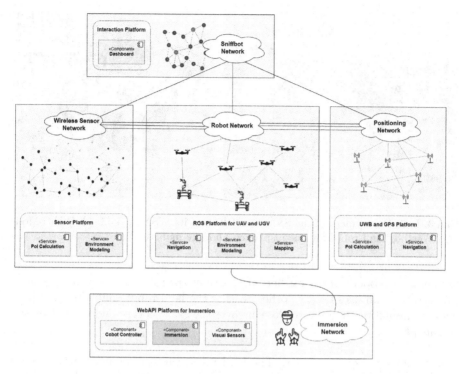

Fig. 2. The networks of the SNIFFBOT fog, their interfaces, services and interactions.

2.1 The Robot Network

Immersive mobile manipulation in dangerous work environments requires several sensoric and actuatoric components, as we have shown in previous work [3,4,42]. At the moment, the Robot Network consists the following specific configuration.

The Land Robot for Tele-Inspection and Tele-Manipulation. The land robot (Fig. 3 right) is a four-wheel drive *Warthog* outdoor robot[2], on which three robot arms have been mounted to enable *immersion* (2 UR5e arms to the left and right and 1 UR3 arm in the middle). The middle UR3 arm carries a camera whose stream is displayed in the VR glasses of the remote *immersion operator*. This camera is controlled by the head of the immersion operator, following its movements, and enables her to guide the immersion and change the direction of inspection, as in [42] (Sect. 3.4). This enables the immersion operator to orient herself easily when inspecting different corners of the remote area. Using a 3-D-Environment Model (Sect. 3.3), the land robot is able to approach a PoI either autonomously or by human navigation (navigation phase). For local detection of the environment, the land robot is additionally equipped with Light Detection And Ranging (LiDAR) sensors and other camera systems. Once, a PoI is reached,

---

[2] https://www.clearpathrobotics.com; arms mounted by https://mybotshop.de.

Fig. 3. Left: Deployment of the SNIFFBOT IRC and its WSN in the field. Right: Modified Warthog land robot for tele-inspection and tele-manipulation.

the immersion operator orients herself, positions the robot in the scene (*last-mile immersion*), and uses the two other arms of the land robot enable tele-gripping and -manipulation, in order to close or cover the gas leak that had been identified (repair phase).

Drones Discovering Gas Leaks. The land robot can communicate with drones surveying the area from above. On these drones, gas sensors can be mounted so that peak points in the distribution of the target gas can be identified in the Environment Model (Fig. 4). One unique selling point of our sensors is that they employ nanomaterials as sensing elements enabling the integration of a lightweight and versatile gas sensing platform (Sect. 3.2). While we have experimented mainly with Ammonia and Hydrogen Sulfide, many other molecules can be sensed after a specification, sensor chip design, and testing phase.

Fig. 4. Drones for finding gas leaks from above. Spectrometer-based sensor board (green) is mounted on the drone. FPGA controller on top (pink board). (Color figure online)

The drone system should be able to explore large areas. As large-bandwidth real-time wireless communication can become very expensive in terms of energy consumption, an edge-controller computer on the drone is desirable. However, this poses a significant challenge since the drone controller system integrates many algorithms, including sensing, perception, localization, decision making, control, etc., for which large amounts of data in real-time need to processed. This data is highly heterogeneous and requires accurate spatial and temporal synchronization as well as pre-processing. Additionally, the space and energy available onboard the drone are limited which significantly restricts the drone's capabilities for 3D sensing, localization, navigation, and path planning tasks.

It is, therefore, essential to choose an energy-efficient edge-controller computer for the drone. FPGAs provide the energy-efficient task processing required for the drone [16,19,21,41]. FPGAs are often built into small systems with few memory. They can process massively parallel computations and make use of the properties of perception (e.g., ICP for LiDAR scan matcher [7]), localization (e.g., Kalman filter), and controlling kernels (e.g., autonomous flight controller) to remove additional logic and simplify the implementation. FPGAs can, therefore, meet real-time requirements while achieving high energy efficiency compared to CPUs and GPUs (Sect. 4.2).

One of the novelties of the SNIFFBOT is that it combines a WSN for sniffing and positioning with drone services and land robots. To autonomously navigate to a PoI, the IRC uses the PoI calculation service, which, in turn, relies on the WSN (Fig. 2, left) and the Positioning Network (Fig. 2, right) to work properly. We have explored three scenarios how the drones communicate with these networks in the SNIFFBOT fog:

Singular Sniffing. The chemiresistive-based nano-sensor is a drone component, but is not a node of the WSN. Then, the drone is solely integrated in the Positioning Network (Sect. 4.2).

Sensor node dropping. A node of the WSN is loosely attached to the drone, but independent of the drone. Then, the drone is integrated in the Positioning Network, while the sensor node is integrated into the WSN, but they are coupled by their common position in space. In this scenario, the drone could drop the sensor node into the field (dropping phase), deploying the WSN permanently into the field (Sect. 4.2).

Sensor-drone integration. The WSN node is integrated as a drone device, and the drone is integrated in the Positioning Network. Then, communication and services run via the drone, and serve WSN as well as Positioning Network. (Sect. 3.1).

2.2   The Self-organizing, Sniffing Wireless Sensor Network

In recent years, WSNs are broadly used in different applications, such as industry monitoring [27,45], disaster detection and rescue [11,13], and health care [12,28]. Especially in hazardous environment, combined with Unmanned Aerial Vehicless (UAVs) and robots, a WSN can cover large area and provide multi-dimensional views of PoI, which cannot be achieved by a single or few UAVs and robots alone.

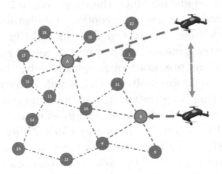

Fig. 5. Drones and WSN complement each other for sniffing and localization. Gateway sensor nodes in green. (Color figure online)

Before starting to sniff, the SNIFFBOT sensor nodes have to self-organize to set up a well-connected WSN. To this end, they run a self-organization protocol. During self-organization, the topology of the WSN depends on the nodes' communication range as well as the deployment environment, but the predominant traffic flow is directed towards a single base station. As far as multi-hop communication is concerned, the network can be organized either flat – where all nodes play similar roles (namely, sensing and packet forwarding) – or hierarchical, where the nodes are organized into multiple clusters and in each cluster, one of the nodes is designated as a cluster head. A flat topology is easier to set up but it is inefficient, as communication is carried out hop-by-hop, involving packet flooding or gossiping [10]. A hierarchical topology, on the other hand, is difficult to set up, requiring global decisions to be made pertaining to the number of cluster heads needed to connect the entire network and the duration of a period during which nodes serve as cluster heads. For our case, neither model is optimal due to the involvement of the mobile agents. To speed up data collection, it is more feasible to dynamically designate one or more nodes as gateways with which the robots and UAV interact, as shown in Fig. 5, in which case the remaining nodes should forward packets to these gateways.

2.3   The Positioning Network

According to the current state of the art, no localization technology is suitable for both indoor and outdoor environments.

Outdoor. In outdoor mode, Global Positioning System (GPS) modules are attached to the exploration mobile agents for field operations. When placing a WSN node in the field during the dropping phase, its position can be computed from and permanently fixed to the GPS position. On the other hand, during exploration with a sniffer drone, the sensor position varies with the drone position. In outdoor mode, Simultaneous Localisation and Mapping (SLAM) algorithms and PoI calculation are computed in the same GPS coordinate system, which, however, lacks precision for fine-grain operations. To increase the accuracy from a few meters to 1–3 cm, SNIFFBOT uses the service "Hochpräzise Echtzeit-Positionierungs-Service (HEPS)", available via ntrip.de from Staatsbetrieb Geobasisinformation und Vermessung Sachsen (GeoSN). In addition, the position of the WSN node can be calculated via the Robot Operating System (ROS) service Transform (TF) with an accuracy of few millimeters.

Indoor. In buildings, we use SLAM with autonomous Ultra-wideband (UWB) transceivers from decawave.com equipped with rechargeable batteries. Using a fixed UWB positioning network for emergency scenarios is discussed in [23]. The UWB modules calculate distances to each other in 3 dimensions. Thus, both UWB and WSN nodes must be placed in the building for navigation and monitoring. When the land robot is equipped with a UWB node, it can navigate in the UWB coordinate system and create maps with SLAM algorithms.

2.4   The Immersion Network

Immersion in the SNIFFBOT collective consists of two tasks, tele-inspection and tele-operation. To this end, a specific immersion network is realized in the SNIFFBOT fog. The success of the tele-operations depends on the quality of the data extracted from the physical environment, the quality of the Virtual Reality (VR), and the quality of the coordination between the human operators and the robots. In particular, the robots must have precise, sensitive, and stable end manipulators that enable force-dependent operations, and their force-feedback mechanism should provide real-time and intuitive experience. Mimicking the movements of a human by a remote robot can be seen as human avatars with tactile abilities [14]. In SNIFFBOT IRC, the robotic avatars possess human-sized limbs which facilitates remote sensing and control (Sect. 4.3).

2.5   Coordination of the Sniffbot IRC via Dashboard

When the facility to be monitored is complex, employing a large number of mobile agents is critical. For example, significant gas leaks at multiple locations require multiple interventions. Likewise, the physical environment may be too large to be monitored with a single or a handful of mobile agents. Consequently, an efficient and seamless coordination between the mobile agents and the remote human operators is critical. In this regard, the *IRC dashboard* can be useful to provide an overview of environmental monitoring and analysis, as well as to help to decide when to switch between different robot control techniques. Therefore, the SNIFFBOT collective has a desktop-based dashboard to be inspected by a second operator, the *dashboard operator*, who talks to the immersion operator to manage all situations in the field of operation.

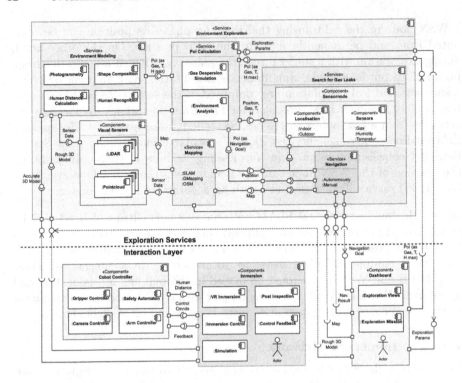

Fig. 6. Overview of the service architecture.

3   Service Architecture of a Sniffing Immersive Robot Collective

This section presents several of the basic services that support the 4 major innovations of the SNIFFBOT collective in more detail (Fig. 6): (a) the big artificial nose is enabled by a self-organizing sniffing WSN, built from sensor nodes (Sect. 3.1), (b) the nano-nose is a sensor array sensing with nano-materials (Sect. 3.2), (c) the 3-D nose needs a 3-D Environment Model service (Sect. 3.3) with a PoI discovery service, (d) and the mobile human avatar relies on the Immersive Control service for tele-inspection and -manipulation (Sect. 3.4).

3.1   The Big Nose: Sniffing Services of Wireless Sensor Network

In the following, we describe the most important services of the WSN and its sensor nodes to establish a big nose for the SNIFFBOT collective. Every sensor node contains gas nano-sensors described in Sect. 3.2. The gas sensors could be heterogeneous and may have different configurations, like measurement time and sampling rates.

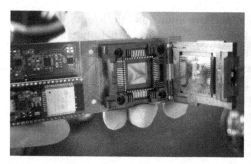

Fig. 7. Left: Nano-sensor array to detect Ammonia gas. Right: Wireless sensor node integrating an array of nano-sensors to detect Ammonia.

The Sensor Node. The sensor node is responsible for managing the gas sensors. It implements a simple threshold-based alarm algorithm to alert the event of a gas leakage. The main functionality of the sensor node platform is to periodically report sensor data via multi-hop communication, via the gateways, to the base station, a remote server in the SNIFFBOT Dashboard (Sect. 3.3). To address the link dynamics, an efficient link quality estimation and topology control algorithm is employed in the communication protocol. During the network setup phase, the network management component is responsible for constructing the topology of the sensor network autonomously.

Besides the nano-sensor array (Fig. 7 left and Fig. 7 right, bottom), the sensor node is equipped with wireless communication services (Fig. 7 right), a battery (on top), and the microcontroller module (in the middle). The microcontroller is responsible for sensor fusion, i.e., for aggregating, pre-processing and sending the sensor data (e.g., visual data, temperature, or gas concentration) to the PoI calculation service (Sect. 3.3).

Detecting Gases with the WSN in Time. The time elapsed from the detection of a concentration of toxic gas surpassing a predefined threshold to the notification of this event to the control station is defined as the System's Response Time (SRT). Most oil refinaries set this limit to 20 s [9]. This time is affected by the efficiency of the data collection algorithm, the time the mobile agents take to establish contact with the remote control station, and the quality of the wireless link between the mobile agents and these stations. The time a source node takes to report an interesting event is a function of the hop-distance of the source node from the nearest gateway and can be known only in a probabilistic sense, as the interesting event may occur anywhere in the deployment environment. The data collection algorithm should prioritize packet transmission to give precedence to nodes which detect interesting events, thereby minimizing the overall delay. The time a mobile agent takes to report the interesting event to a remote control station is also a random variable, since the mobile agent may not be located at or near a gateway.

An upper limit on the SRT influences how many mobile agents should be dispatched to interact with the wireless sensor network. An important factor in this sense is the size and complexity of the civil structure to be monitored. If multiple mobile agents are deployed, multiple gateways should be designated and a more complex coordination is required to aggregate the sensor data. On the other hand, using higher number of mobile agents, the resolution of gas dispersion and concentration can be refined so that more accurate and faster identification of PoIs is possible.

3.2   The Nano-Nose: Sensing with Nano-Sensors

The nano-nose of SNIFFBOT, available in every sensor node, relies on an array of gas sensors integrated in multiplexing circuits for multiple and reliable detection facilitate sensing. It can be mounted on a sniffing mobile robot, a sniffing drone, or deployed at fixed locations.

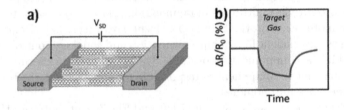

Fig. 8. (a) Operating principle of CNT based chemiresistive gas sensor and (b) electrical resistance monitoring.

Regarding high sensitivity needs, nanomaterials are ideal candidates to be used as sensing material in an electrical format due to their high surface-to-volume ratio, which allows conductivity modulation of the complete bulk of the material as a result of the attachment of few gas molecules on the surface which can be tailored for each specific gas. CNTs have been used in a chemiresistor format, given their excellent electron transport [15] and mechanical properties that enable the fabrication of highly sensitive sensors on flexible and light-weight supports, appropriate for the integration on small robots with low loading capacity. In this context, chemiresistive sensing is an appropriate format due to its low power consumption and simplicity in structure and fabrication. The operating principle is based on the modification of CNTs' electrical properties as a result of the interaction with gas molecules. A low voltage is applied between two metal electrodes connected by a CNT network while the change in electrical resistance is monitored upon exposure to the target gas (Fig. 8).

In this project, we have demonstrated the highly sensitive, selective and self-validating detection of target gases (NH_3 and H_2S) using a small footprint multichannel sensing platform based on Single-Walled Carbon NanoTubes (SWCNTs) (Fig. 7 left) [31,32]. Binding of NH_3 on the CNT's sidewall defects causes a charge carrier depletion and therefore an increase of electrical resistance. In the case of H_2S detection, a prior functionalization of the CNTs with gold nanoparticles creates binding points for interaction with the sulfur atom of the gas. The binding lowers the work function of the gold nanoparticles [29], resulting in an electron donation into the CNT and ultimately affecting its conductivity.

As the requirement for precision increases, the needed spatial resolution becomes smaller, while the mathematical complexity, physical detail, and computational cost required to perform accurate simulations increase. Many models have already been proposed in the literature to describe the function of a CNT sniffing process. For instance, the resistance of a CNT in [8] is modeled as

$$R = \frac{L}{S \cdot \sigma} \tag{1}$$

where L is the length of the CNT, σ is the conductivity and S is the section of the CNT. The conductivity can be written as a function of the carrier concentrations n & p and mobilities μ_n & μ_p as follows:

$$\sigma = q(n\mu_n + p\mu_p) \tag{2}$$

We have proposed a signal processing Cellular Nonlinear Network (CNN) for the detection and classification of experimental measurements resulting from manufactured memristive gas sensor matrix. The developed CNN with the gas sensors together forms an intelligent selective gas sensors system that can discriminate between hazardous Ammonia and Hydrogen Sulfide gases. This system can not only classify the detected gases reliably but also helps to determine their concentration levels.

3.3   The 3-D Nose: The Environment Model Service

Navigating in complex environments requires two things: Firstly, the environment must be captured in sufficient detail, whereby the most varied sensor information, including our sniffing sensors, must be bundled in a spatial model. Secondly, for precise robot manipulation tasks (such as gripping objects) or using fine-grained objects), precise movements must be made. Both models consist of 3-D point clouds, whose individual entries correspond to details from the environment.

Rough 3-D Environmental Model. The *rough environmental model* is required by almost all sub-tasks for autonomous navigation. In general, a spatial model can be created by recognizing pre-specified, *coded targets* from several images by reconstructing a scene in three dimensions via triangulation. This procedure corresponds to a passive stereo/multi-image acquisition and processing. The result is a minimalistic but highly accurate point cloud [34]. However, for the rough environment model no coded targets are available, because the SNIFFBOT wheeled robot manoeuvers in unknown terrain.   The rough environment model with

Fig. 9. The online inspection 3-D Environment Model of SNIFFBOT.

the corresponding point cloud for navigation will be calculated, for all our components, on a single ROS node. Therefore, the point cloud will be limited to absolutely necessary information and will not be suitable for immersive visualization. For an immersive parallel or subsequent assessment of the environment by experts with a state-of-the-art VR goggle, a dense and, if possible, meshed and textured environment model is helpful. Details of a scene not covered by the rough environment model, or details whose uncertainties are still very large, can be investigated in this way. Additionally, sensor information for gases and noises has to be integrated into the VR information. For such an *inspection environment model* (Fig. 9), the computational effort is much higher compared to the rough environment model, so that the data must be calculated separately.

Fine-Grained 3-D Environmental Model. For the fine-grained, partial spatial model, the movement of the robot arms can be measured, based on coded targets, with micrometre accuracy using the self-developed photogrammetry toolkit [34]. Through the comparison with the executed motion path, corrections on positions and movements can be implemented in the robot control system, which improves the accuracy of the arm movement of the SNIFFBOT platform. From our point of view, a precise movement within the surroundings requires a (dense) point cloud of high accuracy. For this purpose, specific algorithms for pattern projection are required whose results should be compared with passive and evenly-illuminated stereo-image systems, as well as a mono-image system on axis six of a handling robot arm.

Services for Discovering PoIs. Based on the received sensor data and the Mapping Service, the PoI calculation service computes suitable simulation models to create heat and gas dispersion maps. Using these simulation-generated maps, it

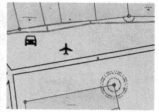

Fig. 10. Left: Using with SLAM created map. Center: While creating a map with SLAM. Right: PoI on the 2-D GPS-based world map from openstreetmap.org, with the sensed intensity of gas.

returns resulting PoIs to the drones and robots. The simulation models will be updated continuously as new data arrives. Two main services are delivered:

Detection. By collecting sensor readings in heat maps and complementing them with simulated data, hot spots representing PoIs can be identified in the environment. In chemical production plants, current anomalies as well as alerting gas concentrations and simulation-based dispersion forecasts can be reported early to trigger appropriate reactions. Hence, further damage and hazardous accidents are prevented.

Reaction. The PoI calculation service will also recommend actions by sending PoIs to the robot network. Investigating these points will improve maps and simulations, thereby contribute in forecasting the dispersion of gases and tracking their sources. In case of detected anomalies, appropriately prioritized notifications will be sent to the Immersive Control and the Dashboard. Then, the human operators can decide whether the Warthog land robot should be sent out to fix the leaks and malfunctions [24].

The Mapping and Navigation Service of the Robot Collective. Using the WSN and the Positioning Network, the Mapping Service can calculate a 2-D world map using a SLAM algorithm (Fig. 10 left, center). On this map, PoI can be entered by the Positioning Network (Fig. 10 right). In outdoor mode, also GPS-world maps may be used for coarse-grain localization.

To navigate to the PoIs in the environment, the land robot has three possible options:

Manual navigation. The land robot is manually moved by the dashboard operator,
Manual navigation by immersion operator. The land robot is manually moved by the immersion operator,
Autonomous navigation. The robot navigates autonomously to the PoIs.

In the first and second case, the maneuvering will be coordinated with the video stream by one of the operators, while the Environment Model (Sect. 3.3)

Fig. 11. An immersion operator with its sensors.

will only be used for collision avoidance. In the third case, the 2-D world map and the 3-D Environment Model will be used for navigation (Sect. 3.3). In the third case, the search for a route can be supported by an existing 2-D world map, e.g., a map of an industrial plant. In any case, positions should be calculated as precise as possible to enable precise last-mile immersion.

The Navigation of the SNIFFBOT *Drone System.* The SNIFFBOT's drone subsystem needs an off-board and on-board component to work. The former consist on the communication of the PoI Discovery Service, as well as a ground station, with a monitoring display and a manual controller in the hands of an operator. Safety rules requires that, when the drone is in autonomous-flight mode, an operator must use a manual controller to monitor and safeguard the drone. The on-board module is in charge of the drone's planning and control which discharges wireless communication. The autonomous navigation services consist of two back-end localization modules; the ICP scan matcher, which uses only data from the LiDAR, and the EKF (Extended Kalman Filter) that fuses all the data to get a correct 3-D localization. At the moment, the drone is only capable of relative positioning for indoor navigation. Some of the on-board services are offloaded on the drone's FPGA, which is explained in Sect. 4.2.

3.4   The Mobile Human Avatar: Services for Immersive Control

The specific field of robot control embedded in VR is still young [26], in particular if an avatar should be mobile. A human operator shall "dive" into a remote environment by tele-inspecting it, tele-operating a remote robot and tele-controlling its movements. The more seamless the audio-visual interaction, the deeper is the immersion experience [38].

Immersive Control of Robots. In SNIFFBOT, immersion is achieved with a VR application that uses one or several video streams from cameras placed on the middle robot arm of the SNIFFBOT mobile platform. If the immersion operator wish to see a different perspective, she may turn her head which causes the camera to be turned in the same way (Fig. 11, upper left). The SNIFFBOT operator is equipped with Oculus Rift S VR glasses[3]. To track head motion, the pose of the VR glasses is used. We use as input from the remote scene the image stream and pointcloud of a Rubedos VIPER camera[4]. The VIPER camera is mounted on the middle UR3 arm of the Warthog and mimics the movement of the head of the immersion operator.

Additional sensors, such as wearable sensors attached to the operator's arms, body and head, are useful for tracking the movements of the operator and for guiding the movement of the robot arms [42] (Fig. 11, upper right). We use 3 Bosch XDK sensors[5] each on the left and right arm of operator to calculate poses of the palms of the hands. On the remote scene, the trajectories calculated from these poses mimick the operator's movements by two UR5e arms. For instance, to enable accurate manipulation of objects, the immersion operator can be equipped with haptic output devices providing feedback from the remote scene. HaptiGuard are belts with vibration motors placed on the arms [33] that provoke tactile sensing on the skin of the immersion operator, for instance, if she moves too fast (Fig. 11, upper right).

For tele-manipulation, to carry out precise mechanical tasks with variable force, such as to grip the lock a valve, to fix a screw, or to check a mechanical connection for its stability, tele-manipulation capabilities are essential. Figure 11, lower left, shows a immersive operator with SenseGlove[6] gloves on, closing a Robotiq 2F[7] and 3F gripper[8] mounted on the arms of the SNIFFBOT. In addition to tracking finger position, these gloves also enable haptic feedback in form of varying resistance to finger movements. The movement of the fingers of the operator are recognized and transported to the gripper, where they are replayed. Figure 11, lower right, shows a immersive operator with gloves on, closing a gripper around a plastic bottle.

Simulation Service for Immersion Control. For stability, every bit of the implementation must first be thoroughly tested in a simulation with software-in-the-loop (SIL). For this purpose, existing simulation tools for ROS can be used, e.g., Gazebo or MoveIt [17, Chapter 4,6]. In our case, almost all immersion control robot components had ready-made Gazebo configurations. The challenge, however, was to compose these components into an overall robotic software system. Another challenge was to integrate motion planning with ROS MoveIt for the

---

[3] https://www.oculus.com/rift-s/features/.

[4] https://rubedos.com/solutions/viper.

[5] https://developer.bosch.com/products-and-services/sdks/xdk/develop/c/technical-information.

[6] https://www.senseglove.com/developer/.

[7] https://robotiq.com/products/2f85-140-adaptive-robot-gripper.

[8] https://robotiq.com/products/3-finger-adaptive-robot-gripper.

robot arms with the immersion control system. This is necessary for collision detection when several arms are controlled simultaneously. With this configuration we are now able to simulate the immersive control system under development without having to adapt the simulation.

4   Experiments with the IRC Fog Services

To evaluate the feasibility of the SNIFFBOT innovations and the approach in general, we experimented with the service architecture after deploying the IRC on an open field (Fig. 3 right).

4.1   Sniffing with a Big Nose

The current implementation of SNIFFBOT consists of the Warthog robot (Fig. 3 left), a WSN with sensor nodes with arrays of high sensitive Ammonia nano-sensors, and a Positioning Network. The WSN is able to achieve a high degree of spatio-temporal sensing, whereas the mobile robot sniffs dangerous gases in its immediate environment. The Positioning Network analyses data according to its deployment and identifies a PoI. Also, it coordinates with the mobile robot to navigate to the region of interest.

The WSN consists of 5 Zolertia RE-Mote revision B motes[9], forming a rectangular topology with one of the sensor nodes deployed at the center of the rectangle. To each sensor node, a 64-channel Ammonia nano-sensor is connected via a serial communication bus (Fig. 7). The sensor nodes are powered by a power bank and sample their environment at a rate 1 Hz. The node in the middle of the field serves as a gateway between the sensor network and the PoI Calculating Service using the MQTT protocol [22] over a WiFi link.

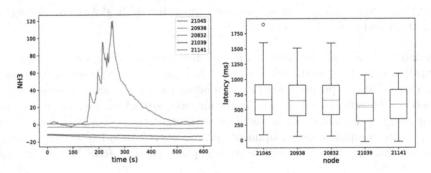

Fig. 12. Left: Samples of NH_3 measurements. Right: The end-to-end communication latency of the wireless sensor network.

---

[9] https://zolertia.io/product/re-mote/.

Latency. We placed a bottle containing Ammonia at one of the sensor nodes. Figure 12 shows the gas fluctuation when a significant Ammonia concentration was released into the air. We set up a threshold of 40% relative resistance change to trigger a PoI event and defined the end-to-end communication latency as the difference between the time at which the gas sensors detect an interesting event and the time at which the events arrive at the PoI Detection Service. Figure 12 shows the boxplot of the end-to-end communication latency for the 5 sensor nodes. The green dash lines represent the mean value and the orange lines denote the median. We observed that on average, the end-to-end latency was below 750 ms.

Figure 13 shows the overall system response latency, which is defined as the time elapsed between the first gas sensor reading an interesting event and a mobile agent received the corresponding PoI event. The maximum system response latency was ca. 1600 ms, while the minimum was ca. 678 ms.

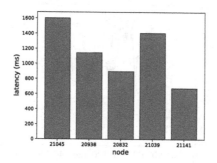

Fig. 13. The overall system response latency.

4.2   Sensing with a Drone

The SWCNT-based sensing platform was successfully integrated into the drone system and the sensing performance in real operational conditions was tested using a 25% Ammonia solution as gas source. The results are presented in Fig. 14. The sensing response showed good stability while the drone was standing on the floor with the propellers on and a slight drift while approaching the gas source (Fig. 14a). A noticeable increase of around 50% was observed when the drone approached the gas source indicating the interaction of Ammonia gas molecules with SWCNTs (Fig. 14b). Then, the sensing response fluctuated while the drone hovered on top of the gas source demonstrating a reliable detection despite the air vortex created by the propellers (Fig. 14c). Finally, the response decreased when the drone was flown away from the gas source (Fig. 14d).

FPGA-based Drone Flying. SNIFFBOT's drone system implements several robust localization and controller algorithms for stable flight operation using a PYNQ-Z1 board with a Xilinx Zynq-7000 SoC device combining the programmable logic

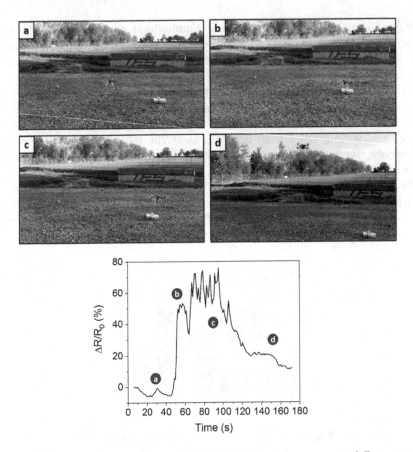

Fig. 14. Average sensing response of the SWCNT-based sensors at different stages during the drone sensing experiment. (a) Drone flying statically before sensing. (b) Drone flying directly on top of the gas source. (c) Drone hovering above the gas source. (d) Drone flying away from the gas source.

of an FPGA with a dual-core ARM Cortex-A9 processor. The heavy computational loads of this system are the *ICP scan matcher* and the *Model Predictive Controller (MPC)* [20]. The latter has a continuous model (nonlinear system) and uses a simultaneous solution and optimization approach to determine, at each sampling time, an optimal trajectory of the open-loop variable of the model. The parallelism of the FPGA is exploited to comply with the drone's real-time constraints, achieving a control loop frequency 5 Hz and a mean execution time of ≈180 ms. Compared to software-only solutions, this is quite favorite: a 5 Gen i3 processor needs 162 ms and an ARM-A9 core 6 s, while both processors run at a higher clock frequency than the FPGA accelerator and spend much more energy.

4.3 Coupling Autonavigation and Last-Mile Immersion

During our experiments with indoor and outdoor navigation, the hypothesis could be validated that last-mile immersion is quite important because it is not easy to autonomously position the Warthog in front of the gas leak so that, subsequently, it can also autonomously repair the leak. One reason is that the position needed for repair is not always known at PoI identification time. Also, if obstacles have to be bypassed during robot navigation, the orientation at the physical PoI may be different from the orientation calculated, and another autonomous navigation for correction might delay the start of the repair considerably. Also, it is may not possible to automatically position the actuators at the PoI because the leak consists of a larger slit or several holes in a pipe, for which several different Warthog poses for manipulation are required. For these reasons, we interrupt the navigation 1 m before the PoI and let the immersion operator control the Warthog with a joystick for the last mile.

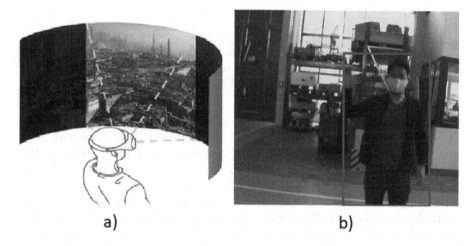

a)   b)

Fig. 15. Immersion View. a) View of the stream screen in VR glasses, b) Screen with human recognized bounding boxes

VR-based Tele-Inspection. Figure 15 a) shows the operator's perception during tele-inspection. The observed image rotates in the VR scene depending on the pose of the VIPER camera and the head of the operator. As VIPER moves, the viewed image also shifts in the operator's vision. This enables her to intuitively estimate the pose of camera in the remote environment. In addition, the operator can recognize humans in the remote environment more quickly with help of bounding boxes, e.g., when searching for injured persons in a buried area (Fig. 15 b)). For the VR, we need minimum quality requirements of 1280×360 px and 30 fps. Network configurations and image compression allow us setup a stable video stream from the VIPER camera to the VR goggles with our minimum requirements. Image compression reduces the network bandwidth consumption by 93% to 96%.

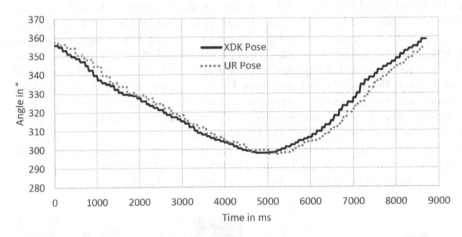

Fig. 16. Delay of UR5e arm on movement of XDK sensor. XDK Pose shows the sensor data from tracking, UR pose shows the delayed UR5e movement. Data is recorded synchronously on the operator-PC connected to XDK and UR5e via WLAN.

Tele-Operating the Arms. Tele-operation should not be delayed too much, in order to keep local and remote scene in synchronisation. Therefore, we have measured the delay of move-and-replay during arm positioning. Figure 16 shows the deviation of the movement of an UR5e arm from the movement of an XDK sensor value. The measurement includes motion tracking, data transmission of the control command to the Warthog, control robot and data transmission of robot pose back to the operator PC; motion planning and delays from accelerations are not considered here. Thus, the measurement indicates how an immersion operator perceives the delay. Figure 16 shows a rotation of one UR5e joint, showing a movement in one direction (X-axis from 0–5 s) and then in the opposite direction (5–9 s), with an angle depicted in the Y-axis. In the sequence 0–4.5 s of Fig. 16 an average deviation of the robot to the operator arm position is ≈2.5° with an approximated linear motion of 12°/s. This results in a delay of approx. 210 ms. In addition to this delay, there is the delay for the data transport from the XDK tracking sensor to the operator PC. For sending XDK data, we use the clock rate of 40 ms at which a stable data transmission could be guaranteed. If we add the data transmission delay of 50 ms (ping value), the total delay is ≈300 ms, which is a quite encouraging result for a non-optimized implementation.

5   Comparison to Related Work

Several tasks of a Sniffing IRC have been documented in the literature, but most approaches do not yet use immersion into remote areas. The task of *mobile robot olfaction* has been recognized widely as important application of outdoor robotic systems. Several projects and industrial products illustrate sensoric drones for different gases [30]. SNIFFERROBOTICS is a company selling a drone sniffing methane gas as *Technology as a Service (TaaS)* [36]. SCENTROID offers several more environmental monitoring services [35], as well as ULC Robotics [40].

Projects combining land robots and drones are less frequent. [5] is a project on sniffing robots, not only for detection of gas leaks, but also for measuring gas distribution. The projects, however, do not enclose a human operator in the loop. The project ROBOGASINSPECTOR uses a land robot for sniffing gases [6], but lacks the connection to a WSN as well as immersion. Using a WSN, however, separates the task of sniffing from the tasks of mapping and navigation, which has the advantage that several gas leaks can be located at the same time. [39] reports about a WSN sensing radiation that is deployed by robots in the field.

Immersive telepresence is, for example, investigated in [2]. Tele-robotics is a specific immersion field with applications in dangerous scenarios. Also the integration of WSN and tele-robots has been attempted before [43], but not for sniffing applications. [18] presents an immersive sniffing system for manufacturing, but does not include mobile agents.

6   Conclusion

In this paper, we have investigated a gas-sniffing immersive robot collective combined with a wireless sensor network for tele-monitoring and tele-operating in dangerous and inaccessible places. In this combination, SNIFFBOT shows how future disaster tele-management systems will look like: SNIFFBOT has a big nose in form of a self-organizing wireless sensor network, it offers nano-material sensing of Ammonia and Hydrogen Sulfide, it can identify gas leaks in a 2-D and 3-D environment model, provides autonomous navigation to these points, and enables the operators to immersively inspect, navigate, and manipulate in the area of danger. The secret of this disaster tele-management system are several innovative fog services which even work without a global infrastructure or power grid. We have presented several experiments with these fog services in the field, showing that sniffing, navigation, tele-inspection and -operation work fine. With regard to toxic gas detection, initial results suggest that the system's overall response time ($SRT \leq 2$ s) is much shorter than the time recommended by the Work Health and Safety Act for Mines and Petroleum Sites of 2013 ($SRT \leq 10$ s) [25]. Alas, since the sniffing IRC is a complex distributed system, many things remain to be investigated. For example, the initialization of the IRC is a very complicated task which is not automated yet, so that experiments with it are difficult to conduct, and studies about the operations of the entire collective are missing. This is an important future work.

Acknowledgment. This work has been supported by the German Federal State of Saxony as part of the "SNIFFBOT: Sniffing Dangerous Gases with Immersive Robots" project under grant agreement number 100369691, by the German Research Foundation

(DFG, Deutsche Forschungsgemeinschaft) as part of Germany's Excellence Strategy - EXC 2050/1 - Project ID 390696704 - Cluster of Excellence "Centre for Tactile Internet with Human-in-the-Loop" (CeTI), as well as by the Federal Ministry of Education and Research of Germany in the programme of "Souverän. Digital. Vernetzt.", joint project 6G-life, project ID 16KISK001K.

References

1. Anderson, A.R.: Top five chemicals resulting in injuries from acute chemical incidents - hazardous substances emergency events surveillance, nine states, 1999–2008. Surveil. Summ. **64**(SS02), 39–46 (2015). https://www.cdc.gov/mmwr/preview/mmwrhtml/ss6402a6.htm
2. Aykut, T.: Towards immersive telepresence: stereoscopic 360-degree vision in realtime. Dissertation, Technische Universität München, München (2019)
3. Aßmann, U., et al.: Cross-layer adaptation in multi-layer autonomic systems (invited talk). In: Catania, B., Královič, R., Nawrocki, J., Pighizzini, G. (eds.) SOFSEM 2019. LNCS, vol. 11376, pp. 1–20. Springer, Cham (2019). https://doi.org/10.1007/978-3-030-10801-4_1
4. Aßmann, U., Piechnick, C., Püschel, G., Piechnick, M., Falkenberg, J., Werner, S.: Modelling the world of a smart room for robotic co-working. In: Pires, L.F., Hammoudi, S., Selic, B. (eds.) MODELSWARD 2017. CCIS, vol. 880, pp. 484–506. Springer, Cham (2018). https://doi.org/10.1007/978-3-319-94764-8_20
5. Bennetts, V.M.H., Kucner, T.P., Schaffernicht, E., Neumann, P.P., Fan, H., Lilienthal, A.J.: Probabilistic air flow modelling using turbulent and laminar characteristics for ground and aerial robots. IEEE Robotics Autom. Lett. **2**(2), 1117–1123 (2017)
6. Bonow, G., Kroll, A.: Gas leak localization in industrial environments using a TDLAS-based remote gas sensor and autonomous mobile robot with the tri-max method. In: IEEE International Conference on Robotics and Automation, pp. 987–992. IEEE, May 2013
7. Censi, A.: An ICP variant using a point-to-line metric. In: 2008 IEEE International Conference on Robotics and Automation, pp. 19–25 (2008). https://doi.org/10.1109/ROBOT.2008.4543181
8. Colasanti, S., Bhatt, V.D., Lugli, P.: 3D modeling of CNT networks for sensing applications. In: 2014 10th Conference on Ph.D. Research in Microelectronics and Electronics (PRIME), pp. 1–4. IEEE (2014)
9. Dargie, W., Chao, X., Denko, M.K.: Modelling the energy cost of a fully operational wireless sensor network. Telecommun. Syst. **44**(1–2), 3–15 (2010)
10. Dargie, W., Poellabauer, C.: Fundamentals of Wireless Sensor Networks: Theory and Practice. Wiley, New Delhi (2010)
11. Erdelj, M., Natalizio, E., Chowdhury, K.R., Akyildiz, I.F.: Help from the sky: leveraging UAVs for disaster management. IEEE Pervasive Comput. **16**(1), 24–32 (2017)
12. Farooqi, M.R., Iqbal, N., Singh, N.K., Affan, M., Raza, K.: Wireless sensor networks towards convenient infrastructure in the healthcare industry: a systematic study. In: Sensors for Health Monitoring, pp. 31–46. Elsevier (2019)
13. Fu, X., Yao, H., Postolache, O., Yang, Y.: Message forwarding for WSN-assisted opportunistic network in disaster scenarios. J. Netw. Comput. Appl. **137**, 11–24 (2019)

14. Haddadin, S., Johannsmeier, L., Diaz Ledezma, F.: Tactile robots as a central embodiment of the tactile internet. Proc. IEEE **107**(2), 471–487 (2019)
15. Han, T., Nag, A., Mukhopadhyay, S.C., Xu, Y.: Carbon nanotubes and its gas-sensing applications: a review. Sens. Actuators A **291**, 107–143 (2019)
16. Jian, M., Lu, Z., Chen, V.C.: Drone detection and tracking based on phase-interferometric Doppler radar. In: 2018 IEEE Radar Conference (RadarConf18), pp. 1146–1149 (2018)
17. Joseph, L., Cacace, J.: Mastering ROS for Robotics Programming - Second Edition: Design, Build, and Simulate Complex Robots Using the Robot Operating System, 2nd edn. Packt Publishing (2018)
18. Jun, M.B., Yun, H., Kim, E.: Human expertise inspired smart sensing and manufacturing. In: 2021 International Conference on Electronics, Communications and Information Technology (ICECIT), pp. 1–7 (2021). https://doi.org/10.1109/ICECIT54077.2021.9641237
19. Kota, F., Zsedrovits, T., Nagy, Z.: Sense-and-avoid system development on an FPGA. In: 2019 International Conference on Unmanned Aircraft Systems (ICUAS), pp. 575–579 (2019)
20. Kouvaritakis, B., Cannon, M.: Model Predictive Control. Springer International Publishing, London (2016). https://doi.org/10.1007/978-0-85729-398-5
21. Kovari, B.B., Ebeid, E.: MPDrone: FPGA-based platform for intelligent real-time autonomous drone operations. In: 2021 IEEE International Symposium on Safety, Security, and Rescue Robotics (SSRR), pp. 71–76 (2021)
22. Light, R.A.: Mosquitto: server and client implementation of the MQTT protocol. J. Open Source Softw. **2**(13), 265 (2017)
23. Lo, A., Yarovoy, A., Bauge, T., Russell, M., Harmer, D., Kull, B.: An ultra-wideband (UWB) ad hoc sensor network for real-time indoor localization of emergency responders. In: Almeida, M. (ed.) Advances in Vehicular Networking Technologies, Chap. 7. IntechOpen, Rijeka (2011). https://doi.org/10.5772/14232
24. Lohse, C., Urbas, L.: Organising a semi-autonomous robot collective: a hybrid approach. In: 26th IEEE International Conference on Emerging Technologies and Factory Automation, ETFA 2021, Vasteras, Sweden, 7–10 September 2021, pp. 1–8. IEEE (2021). https://doi.org/10.1109/ETFA45728.2021.9613522
25. McLean, D.: Response times of gas detectors. NSW Department of Planning and Environment, Resources Regulator (2017). https://www.minex.org.nz/assets/Uploads/Sept-Response-times-of-gas-detectors.pdf
26. Van de Merwe, D.B., Van Maanen, L., Ter Haar, F.B., Van Dijk, R.J.E., Hoeba, N., Van der Stap, N.: Human-robot interaction during virtual reality mediated teleoperation: how environment information affects spatial task performance and operator situation awareness. In: Chen, J.Y.C., Fragomeni, G. (eds.) HCII 2019. LNCS, vol. 11575, pp. 163–177. Springer, Cham (2019). https://doi.org/10.1007/978-3-030-21565-1_11
27. Mikhaylov, K., Tervonen, J., Heikkilä, J., Känsäkoski, J.: Wireless sensor networks in industrial environment: real-life evaluation results. In: 2012 2nd Baltic Congress on Future Internet Communications, pp. 1–7. IEEE (2012)
28. Mohanty, P., Kabat, M.R.: Energy efficient reliable multi-path data transmission in WSN for healthcare application. Int. J. Wireless Inf. Netw. **23**(2), 162–172 (2016)
29. Mubeen, S., et al.: Sensitive detection of H_2S using gold nanoparticle decorated single-walled carbon nanotubes. Anal. Chem. **82**(1), 250–257 (2010)
30. Neumann, P.P., Bennetts, V.M.H., Lilienthal, A.J., Bartholmai, M., Schiller, J.H.: Gas source localization with a micro-drone using bio-inspired and particle filter-based algorithms. Adv. Rob. **27**(9), 725–738 (2013)

31. Panes-Ruiz, L.A., et al.: Selective and self-validating breath-level detection of hydrogen sulfide in humid air by gold nanoparticle-functionalized nanotube arrays. Nano Res. **15**, 2512–2521 (2021)
32. Panes-Ruiz, L.A., et al.: Toward highly sensitive and energy efficient ammonia gas detection with modified single-walled carbon nanotubes at room temperature. ACS Sens. **3**(1), 79–86 (2018)
33. Richardson, M., Thar, J., Alvarez, J., Borchers, J.O., Ward, J., Hamilton-Fletcher, G.: How much spatial information is lost in the sensory substitution process? Comparing visual, tactile, and auditory approaches. Perception **48**(11), 1079–1103 (2019)
34. Riedel, M.: Methodik zur Modellierung von photogrammetrischen Messungen zur Charakterisierung der Genauigkeit von Werkzeugmaschinen. Ph.D. thesis, Technische Universität Dresden, October 2019
35. Scentroid: Scentroid DR 2000 drone-based environmental monitoring (2022). https://scentroid.com/products/analyzers/dr2000-flying-lab/. Accessed 8 Feb 2022
36. Snifferrobotics: Landfill methane emissions (2022). https://www.snifferrobotics.com/snifferdrone. Accessed 8 Feb 2022
37. Tix, M.: Erdgasnetz im Ahrtal steht wieder, December 2021. https://www.energate-messenger.de/news/218008/erdgasnetz-im-ahrtal-steht-wieder. Accessed 8 Feb 2022
38. Tromp, J.G.: Presence, telepresence and immersion: the cognitive factors of embodiment and interaction in virtual environments. Current Biology (1995)
39. Tuna, G., Gulez, K., Mumcu, T.V., Gungor, V.C.: Mobile robot aided self-deploying wireless sensor networks for radiation leak detection. In: 2012 5th International Conference on New Technologies, Mobility and Security (NTMS), pp. 1–5 (2012). https://doi.org/10.1109/NTMS.2012.6208745
40. ULC Robotics: Gas pipeline leak detection drone services (2022). https://ulcrobotics.com/services/uav-gas-leak-detection. Accessed 18 Feb 2022
41. Wan, Z., et al.: A survey of FPGA-based robotic computing. IEEE Circuits Syst. Mag. **21**(2), 48–74 (2021)
42. Werner, S., Falkenberg, J.: A multi-robot for remote piano playing. Technische Universität Dresden, Chair of Software Engineering, Youtube demo video (2017). https://www.youtube.com/watch?v=dO7MNg8BrtA
43. Wichmann, A., Okkalioglu, B.D., Korkmaz, T.: The integration of mobile (tele) robotics and wireless sensor networks: a survey. Comput. Commun. **51**, 21–35 (2014)
44. Wikipedia: Hochwasser in West- und Mitteleuropa 2021. https://de.wikipedia.org/wiki/Hochwasser_in_West-_und_Mitteleuropa_2021
45. Zinonos, Z., Chrysostomou, C., Vassiliou, V.: Wireless sensor networks mobility management using fuzzy logic. Ad Hoc Netw. **16**, 70–87 (2014)

Support for Cloud Applications

Dynamic Threshold Setting for VM Migration

Abdul Rahman Hummaida[✉] , Norman W. Paton , and Rizos Sakellariou

Department of Computer Science, University of Manchester, Kilburn Building,
Oxford Road, Manchester M13 9PL, UK
abdul.hummaida@postgrad.manchester.ac.uk,
{norman.paton,rizos}@manchester.ac.uk

Abstract. Cloud data centres require efficient management of resources
and robust methods that consider SLA violations, node utilisation and
simplify the adaptation decision making process. Thus resource management should be ideally solved in an online manner. To address this,
approaches have been presented in the literature to set thresholds that
trigger VM migration. One challenge with these approaches is they typically use node metrics (e.g., CPU and memory) as an indicator of VM
performance and do not factor in VM performance metrics when setting
the CPU migration threshold. A hypothesis is that migrating VMs without factoring in VM performance metrics, e.g., response time can lead
to either early or delayed migration of VMs. We present an approach to
discover the CPU utilization level for VM migration dynamically. This
approach monitors VM response time and discovers the CPU threshold
where response time would increase beyond a defined SLA level and uses
this threshold for VM migration. We use reinforcement learning (RL) to
learn when it is rewarding to migrate a VM. The RL reward function
drives a policy towards high CPU utilisation and attaches a penalty to
overachieving SLAs. We use simulation to evaluate the approach and
compare it to 4 heuristics: Static, Interquartile Range, Median Absolute
Deviation, Local Regression. The results show a significant reduction in
SLA violations and an increase in CPU utilization of active nodes.

Keywords: Dynamic CPU threshold · Reinforcement Learning · VM
Migration threshold

1 Introduction

Platform as a service (PaaS) is a service model where Cloud Providers (CPs) provide hardware, software stacks and runtime environments for application development. Customers have control over the development environment, including
configuration. CPs host the hardware and software on its infrastructure and
remove the need for customers to maintain the application stack, runtime environments, operating systems and databases. To provide high levels of availability

© IFIP International Federation for Information Processing 2022
Published by Springer Nature Switzerland AG 2022
F. Montesi et al. (Eds.): ESOCC 2022, LNCS 13226, pp. 31–46, 2022.
https://doi.org/10.1007/978-3-031-04718-3_2

and reliability, CPs need to adapt the infrastructure regularly, which is typically comprised of VMs.

However, the VM migration process can be expensive, and thus there is a need to balance the benefit with the cost of the migration. This raises the challenge of deciding when VM migration should be invoked to achieve this balance. The constituent parts of VM migration include: (i) node overload detection, (ii) VM selection for migration from the overloaded node, and (iii) VM placement on a different target node. This is shown in Fig. 1. From our earlier work [19], we have assumed that a Management Algorithm (MA) is responsible for deciding how incoming workloads are assigned to infrastructure resources by regularly assessing the satisfaction of such assignments in achieving a given SLA. The time complexity of the MA influences the frequency of this assessment; the lower the complexity, the more frequently the algorithm can be executed. The Management Framework (MF) enables the MA to execute by providing standard functionality, such as hierarchy level management, the scope of the infrastructure under control or aggregation of utilisation metrics. The combined functionality of the MA and MF results in workloads executing on infrastructure nodes and dynamic reassignment of workloads to resources. In this paper, we focus on node overload detection.

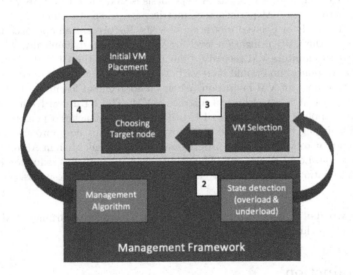

Fig. 1. Cloud Resource Management process

The overload detection methods used in the literature fall onto *reactive*, *proactive* and *hybrid* engagement [20]. Reactive approaches [2,14,30] invoke adaptation when a monitored metric, e.g. CPU utilisation, reaches a specific threshold or when an event is received, such as new VM placement or termination request. Proactive approaches [5,24,33] predict what demands will be placed on the infrastructure and invoke adaptation ahead of the expected resource contention point. Hybrid approaches [4,22] utilise proactive methods and combine these with reactive methods to engage adaptation for long and short term time scales.

The challenge we focus on is in reactive approaches, and these typically use *ad hoc* manually determined policies, such as threshold-based that are popular due to their simplicity. A key element to the threshold-based approach is the assumption there is a high chance that an overload occurs when a node's utilization exceeds the set threshold [1,3,15,25,29,39]. Thus, the threshold level creates an association between a node metric, e.g. CPU utilization, and SLA violation. However, the threshold where SLA violations can occur varies based on the application and the node configuration. Creating a single threshold for all applications and node configurations is incredibly difficult [13]. While the current approaches can reduce overload, they can limit the utilization gains that can be achieved as they leave unused slack for each node. Additionally, threshold approaches can trigger unnecessary migrations as exceeding the set threshold does not necessarily equate to an SLA violation [12]. In addition to heuristics, other techniques have been used for node overload detection; [36] propose a multiobjective optimization that considers the CPU and memory utilization of VMs and nodes. The authors in [37] propose a bio-inspired method based on node susceptibility for host overload detection, and the authors in [29] propose a classical control theory approach.

Application performance is a measure of how well a service performs, and the metrics for measuring this include response time [16,18]. Several CPs have monitoring services, including AzureWatch from Microsoft and CloudWatch from Amazon, that enable monitoring of VM performance hosted on their computing and storage cloud services [16]. We focus on cases where the response time of web-based applications forms part of the SLA between the customer and the CP. The response time can be measured and reported on using the CPs monitoring services.

We hypothesise that including VM performance in the migration decision making will lower the number of SLA violations. In this paper, we incorporate VM response time in a dynamic threshold detection approach and use RL to detect a rewarding threshold level to use by receiving feedback from the VM migration process. The main contributions of this paper are the following:

1. A coordinated migration method that automates the setting of CPU threshold, achieving lower SLA violations and increasing node utilization.
2. A model-free reinforcement learning algorithm for online VM migration that incorporates VM response time in decision making and removes human knowledge to set CPU threshold.
3. Evaluation of the proposed approach using simulation, appropriate workloads and a performance comparison against other approaches in the literature.

The rest of this paper is organised as follows. Section 2 describes related work. Section 3 describes the proposed reinforcement learning algorithm. Section 4 presents an evaluation of our implementation and compares it to four other heuristic dynamic threshold approaches. In Sect. 5, we conclude and discuss future work.

2   Related Work

Reactive approaches are typically implemented using threshold techniques [12] by triggering adaptation when a node's utilization reaches a given level. Beloglazov and Buyya [9] proposed a collection of adaptive policies for setting the upper thresholds: Interquartile Range, Median Absolute Deviation, Local Regression, and Robust Local Regression. The thresholds can be calculated through statistical analysis of historical node utilisation metrics. Other approaches include adaptive heuristic algorithms [39]. The authors in [26] proposed an overload and underloaded node detection. A node is deemed overloaded if the actual and the predicted total CPU usage of 7-time intervals ahead exceed the defined overload threshold. The authors in [25] propose multiple exponential weighted moving average algorithms to detect overloaded nodes. The authors also incorporated a probabilistic approach to counter the uncertainty of the long-term predictions and the cost of applying the VM migration. Other proposals include a regression-based algorithm to create an upper threshold for detecting overload [39]. The approach automatically adjusts the upper CPU utilization threshold based on the historical CPU utilization of the nodes. The authors in [15] use three upper CPU utilization thresholds that are set dynamically based on the conditions of CPU utilization. Other approaches attempted to create a composite metric for overload detection, that combines additional metrics to CPU utilization, such as memory and network BW utilization [1].

However, these approaches did not incorporate VM performance, such as response time in setting the node CPU threshold.

Cloud environments are dynamic and exhibit regular changes in the structure of workloads and access patterns. Aptly, Reinforcement learning (RL) can operate online, learn dynamically from interacting with a changing environment, and use new information to enhance decision making. RL approaches do not require prior knowledge of the optimization model and are not coded explicit instructions relating to which action to take next; instead, they learn actions through feedback from the environment. These features make RL well suited to cloud resource management [27]. RL is utilized in multiple approaches related to cloud resource management [6,10,28,31], and here we focus on some of the approaches in the literature that use RL to reduce the complexity of setting adaptation thresholds.

The authors in [23] aim to remove the need for human knowledge to define adaptation rules by using using a fuzzy rule-based RL algorithm that learns and modifies fuzzy rules at runtime. The author's approach combines Q-learning, an RL algorithm, with fuzzy control where the fuzzy control facilitates human reasoning and the Q-learning allows dynamic rules adjustment. The authors in [7] also aim to adapt the configuration of an application dynamically. They propose to use RL to manage threshold-based rules, where one controller modifies an application configuration, and another monitors the adaptation reward. In contrast to the approach in [23], the author's approach requires human knowledge to initialise the rules.

The authors in [32] propose to manage VM resource configurations by monitoring performance feedback from each VM. The authors aim to optimize the VM performance by learning the VM resource allocation that enhances metrics such as VM response time and throughput by using RL. The reconfiguration process happens periodically on a predefined time interval. A controller fetches the VMs current state and computes valid actions. The RL state is defined as a composite of VM memory size, scheduler credit and the number of virtual CPUs assigned to each VM. The RL method chooses an action and monitors the reward. Actions adjust resources such as the CPU and memory assigned to a VM. The work in [11] proposes CoTuner, for coordinated configuration of VM resources and parameters of their applications. Each VM has an agent that monitors the VM and adapts its configuration to the environment. Reconfiguration actions take place periodically at predefined time intervals. The RL method receives performance feedback and updates the VM and application configuration. For VM configuration, CoTuner can adjust both CPU and memory VM assignments. For applications, CoTuner can change parameter settings.

Similar to our proposed approach, the discussed methods use RL to dynamically change a threshold configuration to optimise performance and reduce SLA violations. In contrast, our approach uses a reduced RL state instead of tracking each VM CPU and memory configuration. We track the node CPU utilization as our primary RL state, resulting in a smaller RL state space and faster convergence compared to approaches with a more dense RL state.

This paper develops an RL-based controller to solve the challenge of determining a node CPU utilization threshold for VM migration and combine Q-Learning with an aggregated state action space to address the curse of dimensionality in Q-learning. We focus on node overload detection and aim to find the CPU utilization at which VM response time will start to degrade beyond a defined SLA target.

3   Proposed Reinforcement Learning Management Algorithm

In our previous work [19], we presented a novel hybrid hierarchical decentralized management framework that rapidly provides the information needed for scale decision making. In this hybrid architecture, higher-level controllers assist lower decentralised controllers. The lowest level controller manages a single node and enables it to be completely autonomous and cooperate with other autonomous nodes to facilitate VM migration. Nodes can receive escalation requests from higher-level controllers to accommodate a migration, and each node can choose to accept or reject these requests.

In this paper, we add an agent that implements our RL approach to each node in the infrastructure and combines this with our previously proposed hybrid hierarchical architecture. This creates RL agents that are both autonomous and cooperate in managing the data centre infrastructure.

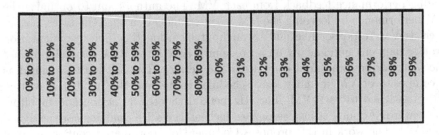

Fig. 2. Granular CPU utilization state

3.1   State

Our goal is to address the challenge of setting a CPU threshold to invoke VM migration. We aim to regularly discover the node CPU utilization that returns the highest reward for performing a VM migration. To achieve this, we need to track nodes CPU state and associate a reward for migrating at each CPU state. However, the granularity of capturing the CPU state is crucial in avoiding the high dimensionality challenge in RL.

We use a state reduction approach and aggregate node state to groups, with each group based on their CPU utilisation, as shown in Fig. 2. By default, we start by creating ten groups, 10% each, using Eq. 1, which creates groups from 0 to 9. For example, State1 means the node state has an average CPU utilisation of 10% to 19%. State6 means the node has an average utilisation between 60% and 69%.

$$stateGroup = \frac{avgCpuUtilization(node)}{stateGroups} \qquad (1)$$

We hypothesise that a fine-grained tracking of CPU utilization between 90% and 100% will enable our RL approach to detect a more optimal migration threshold, compared to a single group for the 90%+ CPU utilization. We apply the fine-grained approach on 90% and above to avoid an increase in the RL state space, which could impact convergence speed.

Periodically, each node additionally classifies the state for all running VMs as *Normal* or *Stressed*, and we use response time as a measure for application performance [17]. To account for variation in response time during the lifetime of an application, we use an approach similar to [28] and apply linear regression on collected response time during each monitoring period. A VM is classed as stressed when the 95th percentile of response time during a monitoring period is above a defined SLA threshold that by default is 500 ms. We categorise the state of VMs as *Normal* when the 95th percentile of the response time is below the defined SLA level. The classification of state occurs during the regular node check. When a VM is stressed, the RL agent always engages the migration mechanism and chooses an action, using the method described in the next section. When VMs are in a normal state, the agent will choose an action using an ϵ-greedy policy [34] to decide if migration should be performed on this node state. This means with a small probability of ϵ, the agent will choose to explore and not exploit by randomly selecting an available action. This leads the agent to learn the node CPU utilization with the highest reward for migration, which the agent exploits in future cycles.

3.2   Actions

Each node contains an RL agent in our architecture that carries out decision making. The RL agent performs actions to achieve QoS metrics and increase infrastructure utilization. As part of the decision making process, an RL agent needs to identify a new target node for the VM being migrated. The RL agent aims to find the actions that maximise reward and chooses a target node based on a CPU utilization group 0 to 9, based on [21]. When the RL agent chooses an action target2, it means migrating the VM to a node with CPU utilisation of 20% to 29%. Once an action is selected, we use a greedy policy to select the first available node that fits the action group. Typically, the agent chooses an action that maximises future reward from the available actions. The agent receives a reward after each action, which is described in the following section. This reward is used to update the node's state-action value pair using Eq. 2 [38], where α is the learning rate and determines how the agent learns from recent updates. γ is the discount factor used to dampen the reward's effect on the agent's choice of action. $MaxQ(s_{t+1}, a_{t+1})$ returns the maximum estimate for the future state-action pair.

$$Q(s_t, a_t) \leftarrow Q(s_t, a_t) + \alpha[r_t + \gamma MaxQ((s_{t+1}, a_{t+1}) - Q(s_t, a_t))] \quad (2)$$

3.3   Reward

The goal for RL is to maximise rewards through incrementally mapping states to actions. We track the achieved response time when the agent takes action at varying levels of CPU utilization and calculate a reward post-action using Algorithm 1. When *currentRT* is a value below or equal to the *TargetRT* and thus satisfying SLA (line 2), we assign varying reward levels. When the action is a no-action (line 3), we give the maximum reward of 1 as no migration cost was incurred and SLA is met. This helps the agent learn that no-action is rewarding for the given node state and dynamically learn the threshold to perform a migration.

When the VM was not meeting its SLA target, as in stressed (line 5), and is now meeting SLA, we want to assign a utility that reflects this as a positive action. Additionally, we want the agent to increase the utilization of target nodes by choosing a target that can host additional VMs and meet SLA. For example, when the TargetRT is 0.5 and the currentRT is 0.4, the reward will be 0.8. When currentRT is 0.3, the reward is 0.6, meaning a higher reward where VMs response time is closest to the target SLA. This has the effect of the RL agent choosing higher utilization target groups.

To learn a dynamic threshold, the RL agent will perform exploratory actions, including no-action and VM migration, using an ϵ-greedy policy to Q. When the agent migrates a VM that is not stressed (line 8), we want to assign a reward that represents closeness to targetRT, with the agent receiving a higher reward when the previousRT of the VM is closest to TargetRT. As we use previousRT in the reward, this iteratively helps the agent learn the node state that maximises reward and thus a threshold for migration. For example, if the agent migrates a non-stressed VM and the previousRT is 0.4, TargetRT is 0.5, then reward is 0.9. This would be a rewarding action for the given node's state. However, a reward of 1 would have been given in a no-action. This would iteratively help the agent discover a dynamic threshold by choosing the more rewarding action.

When *currentRT* is above the *TargetRT* for the VM, thus causing SLA violation, we penalise the action (line 10) by using a clamp function to a maximum of -1. This helps the agent learn the actions that can cause SLA violations, such as migrating to a highly loaded target node or performing a no-action when the source is highly loaded. By receiving a negative reward, the agent learns the node state, thus threshold, that cause SLA violation.

Algorithm 1 helps the agent to learn actions that maximise the reward for a given node state, rewarding actions that meet SLAs, increasing CPU utilization and penalising actions that violate SLAs.

Algorithm 1. VM Reward

1: **procedure** VMREWARD(VM)
2:     **if** currentRT $\leq$ TargetRT   **then**
3:         **if** VM.action == NoAction **then**
4:             reward $\leftarrow$ 1
5:         **if** VM.wasStressed() **then**
6:             reward $\leftarrow \frac{currentRT}{TargetRT}$
7:         **else**
8:             reward $\leftarrow \frac{previousRT}{TargetRT}$
9:     **else**
10:         reward $\leftarrow$ clamp(TargetRT $-$ currentRT, -1)

---

4   Experimental Setup and Evaluation

We use simulation to facilitate the rapid development of experiments of large data centres. We have selected DCSim [35] because of its extensibility. We utilise the hybrid hierarchical decentralized architecture from our earlier work [19], and combine it with a new dynamic threshold detection using RL.

4.1   Experiments

This section evaluates our proposed dynamic threshold discovery approach and its ability to improve SLA violations and node CPU utilization. We consider our proposal under varying workloads and compare our proposal to several overload detection approaches that are effective in the literature. These are Static, Interquartile Range, Median Absolute Deviation, Local Regression. Each of the dynamic threshold approaches [9] is combined with a VM and target selection policy. We additionally compare the proposed approach to our earlier work [21] (RL1). Table 1 shows how we combine these in our experiments.

For workloads, we use public traces included in DCSim: Google 1 and Google 3. Additionally, we use a mixed workload, which comprises traces from Google 1, Google 3, Clarknet and EPA, which are included traces in DCSim. For the RL parameters in Eq. 2, we use $\alpha = 0.5$, and $\gamma = 0.7$ [8].

Table 1. Approaches used in experiments

Comparison Approach	Overload Detection	VM Selection	Target Selection
Static	Static [9]	Highest CPU	Heuristic [9]
IQR	IQR [9]		
MAD	MAD [9]		
LR	LR [9]		
RL 1	VM Response Time [21]	Stressed VM	RL 1
RL 2	VM Response Time & Dynamic Threshold (Proposed)	Stressed VM & Highest CPU	RL 2

4.2   SLA Violations

SLA is the agreement between a CP and a customer and typically specifies a minimum quality of service threshold. In our case, this is VM response time, which we regularly collect for all VMs, and we use it to evaluate if VMs are meeting their SLA targets.

This experiment runs the Google 1, Google 3 and Mixed workloads [35] to evaluate how the stress detection approaches perform on SLA violations. We use

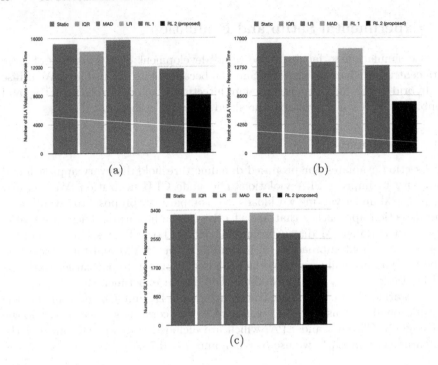

Fig. 3. Number of SLA violations: a) Google 1, b) Google 3, c) Mixed workload

an arrival rate of 90 new applications per hour for this experiment, with each application running for 10 h before shutting down. The experiment simulates 24 h of elapsed time, and we use 500 nodes in this experiment.

The results for Google 1, Google 3 and a mixed workload are shown in Fig. 3a, 3b and 3c respectively and show RL significantly reducing the number of SLA violations for all workloads. On the Google 1 workload, RL2 achieved fewer migrations against all approaches as it incorporates the VM response time and thus directly focuses on controlling the VM performance and migrates VMs when it is close to entering a stressed state. On the Google 3 workload, RL2 achieved fewer migrations than all approaches except RL1, by 12%. On the Mixed workload, RL2 achieved fewer migrations than all approaches except RL1, where it has a comparable number of migrations. The additional migrations in RL2 are due to the exploratory discovery of the migration threshold. They occur at a low probability (ϵ) and tend to be distributed throughout the lifecycle of a VM, and therefore have no impact on SLA violations.

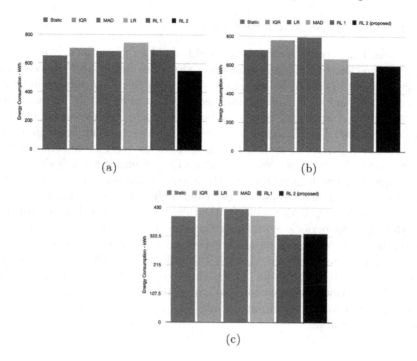

Fig. 4. Energy consumption (KWh): a) Google 1, b) Google 3, c) Mixed workload

4.3   Energy Consumption

The workloads and VM arrival rates, described in the previous section, create a load that requires more than 70% of the CPU resources of active nodes. DCSim can track total energy consumption within the simulated data centre by mapping CPU utilisation of a node to a defined energy consumption amount and tracking this accumulatively for all nodes. The energy consumption results for Google 1, Google 3 and Mixed workload are shown in Fig. 4a, 4b and 4c respectively and show the proposed approach consistently consumed less energy compared to the dynamic threshold heuristics. On the Google 1 workload, our approach (RL2) used 20% less energy than RL1. However, RL2 used 7.9% more energy on the Google 3 workload. This difference is likely due to the number of performed migrations, where RL2 consumes more energy when it performs more migrations, which is the case on the Google 3 workload. This hypothesis is further supported by the result for the mixed workload, where RL1 and RL2 have comparable energy consumption and number of migrations. RL 2 performs some migrations to discover a dynamic threshold, and while these do converge, the discovery process will cause some migration and powering on some nodes, leading to energy consumption. The agent behaviour typically offsets this to increase the utilization of nodes and delay VM close to SLA violations, as exhibited in Google 1, where RL 2 used 27% fewer active nodes than RL1.

4.4   Learning Threshold Assessment

Our approach aims to discover a dynamic threshold for migrations, which delays the migration close to the point where SLA violations would start to occur. Our RL agent aims to perform no-action on VMs up to the point they would enter a stressed state and accumulate reward as described in Sect. 3.3. Figure 5 shows the accumulated learning of agents during the Google 3 workload for different states and actions. The RL agent accumulates Q-value through being in a state and executing a particular action, thus a Q-value for every state-action pair at any given time. States visited less frequently will accumulate rewards slower than more frequent states. Figure 5a shows the agent reward for a no-action at CPU utilization 91% and 92%. These are typically higher than the reward the agent receives for migrating at the same CPU utilization, shown in Fig. 5d, and this leads the agent to perform more no-action. As the CPU utilization increases, we examine some variability on the received reward, shown in Figure 5b. This becomes more pronounced on higher CPU utilization levels of 97% and 98% suggesting this is the threshold during this experiment, shown in Fig. 5c. At 99% CPU utilization, the agent receives a negative or low reward for a no-action and a higher reward for performing a migration, and will choose the migration at this CPU utilization.

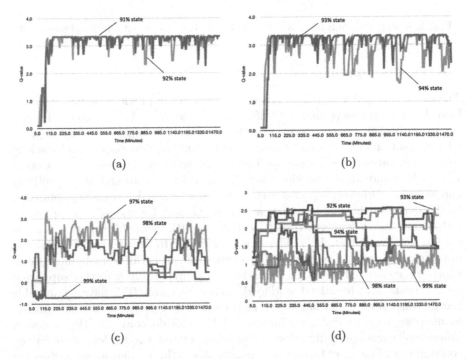

Fig. 5. Q-value for different actions at various CPU utilization levels: a) no-action 91% & 92%, b) no-action 93% & 94%, c) no action 97% to 99%, d) migrations at 90%+

Due to limited space on the paper, we have omitted the results for utilization 0 to 80%. These levels occur more frequently and converge rapidly within a few hours of the learning. This leads our RL agent to execute more no-action and results in fewer VM migrations than the dynamic heuristics.

5   Conclusion and Future Works

This paper proposes a dynamic approach to setting the CPU threshold level used to migrate VMs, using RL. Our approach can learn the migration point dynamically based on the current environment and adjust the migration point when there are changes in the managed environment. Through experimentation, we have shown that the approach can reduce SLA violations and can typically find a more optimal migration point and increase node utilization, compared to four other heuristics from the literature: Static, Interquartile Range, Median Absolute Deviation and Local Regression.

Our approach does not require a model of the environment or managed VMs, making it likely to perform well in executing a range of VMs. However, it is currently limited by using a single dynamic threshold for the entire node, irrespective of the specific behaviour of the individual VMs running on the node. A more robust approach could extend our mechanism and track VMs CPU to relate the properties of the individual VMs to the node's CPU. This could further optimise our proposed method by discovering lower CPU utilization points that reduce SLA violations and higher CPU utilization points that further increase node utilization. We aim to investigate this in future work.

References

1. El-Moursy, A., Abdelsamea, A., Kamran, R., Saad, M.: Multi-dimensional regression host utilization algorithm (MDRHU) for host overload detection in cloud computing. J. Cloud Comput. **8**(1), 8 (2019). https://doi.org/10.1186/s13677-019-0130-2
2. Addis, B., Ardagna, D., Panicucci, B., Squillante, M.S., Zhang, L.: A hierarchical approach for the resource management of very large cloud platforms. IEEE Trans. Dependable Secure Comput. **10**, 253–272 (2013)
3. Alarifi, A., et al.: Energy-efficient hybrid framework for green cloud computing. IEEE Access **8**, 115356–115369 (2020). https://doi.org/10.1109/ACCESS.2020.3002184
4. Ali-Eldin, A., Tordsson, J., Elmroth, E.: An adaptive hybrid elasticity controller for cloud infrastructures. In: 2012 IEEE Network Operations and Management Symposium, pp. 204–212. IEEE, Washington, DC, April 2012
5. Almeida, J., Almeida, V., Ardagna, D., Cunha, Í., Francalanci, C., Trubian, M.: Joint admission control and resource allocation in virtualized servers. J. Parallel Distrib. Comput. **70**, 344–362 (2010)
6. Arabnejad, H., Pahl, C., Jamshidi, P., Estrada, G.: A comparison of reinforcement learning techniques for fuzzy cloud auto-scaling. In: 2017 17th IEEE/ACM International Symposium on Cluster, Cloud and Grid Computing (CCGRID), pp. 64–73 (2017). https://doi.org/10.1109/CCGRID.2017.15

7. Bahati, R.M., Bauer, M.A.: Towards adaptive policy-based management. In: 2010 IEEE Network Operations and Management Symposium - NOMS 2010, pp. 511–518 (2010). https://doi.org/10.1109/NOMS.2010.5488472

8. Barrett, E., Howley, E., Duggan, J.: Applying reinforcement learning towards automating resource allocation and application scalability in the cloud. Concurrency Comput. Pract. Exp. **25**(12), 1656–1674 (2013). https://doi.org/10.1002/cpe.2864

9. Beloglazov, A., Buyya, R.: Optimal online deterministic algorithms and adaptive heuristics for energy and performance efficient dynamic consolidation of virtual machines in cloud data centers. Concurrency Comput. Pract. Exp. **24**, 1397–1420 (2012)

10. Bibal Benifa, J.V., Dejey, D.: RLPAS: reinforcement learning-based proactive autoscaler for resource provisioning in cloud environment. Mob. Netw. Appl. **24**(4), 1348–1363 (2018). https://doi.org/10.1007/s11036-018-0996-0

11. Bu, X., Rao, J., Xu, C.Z.: Coordinated self-configuration of virtual machines and appliances using a model-free learning approach. IEEE Trans. Parallel Distrib. Syst. **24**(4), 681–690 (2013). https://doi.org/10.1109/TPDS.2012.174

12. Dabbagh, M., Hamdaoui, B., Guizani, M., Rayes, A.: An energy-efficient VM prediction and migration framework for overcommitted clouds. IEEE Trans. Cloud Comput. **6**(4), 955–966 (2018). https://doi.org/10.1109/TCC.2016.2564403

13. Dutreilh, X., Kirgizov, S., Melekhova, O., Malenfant, J., Rivierre, N., Truck, I.: Using reinforcement learning for autonomic resource allocation in clouds: towards a fully automated workflow. In: 7th International Conference on Autonomic and Autonomous Systems (ICAS 2011), Venice, Italy, pp. 67–74, May 2011. https://hal-univ-paris8.archives-ouvertes.fr/hal-01122123

14. Feller, E., Rilling, L., Morin, C.: Snooze: a scalable and autonomic virtual machine management framework for private clouds. In: IEEE/ACM International Symposium on Cluster, Cloud and Grid Computing (CCGrid), pp. 482–489 (2012)

15. Garg, V., Jindal, B.: Energy efficient virtual machine migration approach with SLA conservation in cloud computing. J. Central South Univ. **28**(3), 760–770 (2021)

16. Ghahramani, M.H., Zhou, M., Hon, C.T.: Toward cloud computing QoS architecture: analysis of cloud systems and cloud services. IEEE/CAA J. Automatica Sinica **4**(1), 6–18 (2017)

17. Ghanbari, H., Simmons, B., Litoiu, M., Barna, C., Iszlai, G.: Optimal autoscaling in a IaaS cloud. In: Proceedings of the 9th International Conference on Autonomic Computing, ICAC 2012, pp. 173–178. Association for Computing Machinery, New York (2012). https://doi.org/10.1145/2371536.2371567

18. Hu, Y., Wong, J., Iszlai, G., Litoiu, M.: Resource provisioning for cloud computing. In: Proceedings of the 2009 Conference of the Center for Advanced Studies on Collaborative Research, CASCON 2009, pp. 101–111. IBM Corp. (2009). https://doi.org/10.1145/1723028.1723041

19. Hummaida, A.R., Paton, N.W., Sakellariou, R.: SHDF - a scalable hierarchical distributed framework for data centre management. In: 2017 16th International Symposium on Parallel and Distributed Computing (ISPDC), pp. 102–111, July 2017. https://doi.org/10.1109/ISPDC.2017.15

20. Hummaida, A.R., Paton, N.W., Sakellariou, R.: Adaptation in cloud resource configuration: a survey. J. Cloud Comput. **5**(1), 1–16 (2016). https://doi.org/10.1186/s13677-016-0057-9

21. Hummaida, A.R., Paton, N.W., Sakellariou, R.: Scalable virtual machine migration using reinforcement learning. J. Grid Comput. (2021, to be published)

22. Iqbal, W., Dailey, M.N., Carrera, D., Janecek, P.: Adaptive resource provisioning for read intensive multi-tier applications in the cloud. Futur. Gener. Comput. Syst. **26**, 871–879 (2011)
23. Jamshidi, P., Pahl, C., Mendonça, N.C.: Managing uncertainty in autonomic cloud elasticity controllers. IEEE Cloud Comput. **3**(3), 50–60 (2016). https://doi.org/10.1109/MCC.2016.66
24. Jung, G., Hiltunen, M.A., Joshi, K.R., Schlichting, R.D., Pu, C.: Mistral: dynamically managing power, performance, and adaptation cost in cloud infrastructures. In: International Conference on Distributed Computing Systems, pp. 62–73. International Conference on Distributed Computing Systems. IEEE, Washington, DC (2010)
25. Kulshrestha, S., Patel, S.: An efficient host overload detection algorithm for cloud data center based on exponential weighted moving average. Int. J. Commun. Syst. **34**(4), e4708 (2021)
26. Minarolli, D., Mazrekaj, A., Freisleben, B.: Tackling uncertainty in long-term predictions for host overload and underload detection in cloud computing. J. Cloud Comput. **6**(1), 4 (2017)
27. Moreno-Vozmediano, R., Montero, R.S., Huedo, E., Llorente, I.M.: Efficient resource provisioning for elastic cloud services based on machine learning techniques. J. Cloud Comput. **8**(1), 1–18 (2019). https://doi.org/10.1186/s13677-019-0128-9
28. Nouri, S.M.R., Li, H., Venugopal, S., Guo, W., He, M., Tian, W.: Autonomic decentralized elasticity based on a reinforcement learning controller for cloud applications. Futur. Gener. Comput. Syst. **94**, 765–780 (2019). https://doi.org/10.1016/j.future.2018.11.049
29. Padala, P., et al.: Adaptive control of virtualized resources in utility computing environments. In: Proceedings of the 2nd ACM SIGOPS/EuroSys European Conference on Computer Systems 2007, EuroSys 2007, pp. 289–302. Association for Computing Machinery, New York (2007). https://doi.org/10.1145/1272996.1273026
30. Quesnel, F., Lèbre, A., Südholt, M.: Cooperative and reactive scheduling in large-scale virtualized platforms with DVMS. Concurrency Comput. Pract. Exp. **25**(12), 1643–1655 (2013)
31. Rao, J., Bu, X., Xu, C.Z., Wang, K.: A distributed self-learning approach for elastic provisioning of virtualized cloud resources. In: 2011 IEEE 19th Annual International Symposium on Modelling, Analysis, and Simulation of Computer and Telecommunication Systems, pp. 45–54 (2011). https://doi.org/10.1109/MASCOTS.2011.47
32. Rao, J., Bu, X., Xu, C.Z., Wang, L., Yin, G.: VCONF: a reinforcement learning approach to virtual machines auto-configuration. In: Proceedings of the 6th International Conference on Autonomic Computing, ICAC 2009, pp. 137–146. Association for Computing Machinery, New York (2009). https://doi.org/10.1145/1555228.1555263
33. Shen, Z., Subbiah, S., Gu, X., Wilkes, J.: CloudScale: elastic resource scaling for multi-tenant cloud systems. In: Proceedings of the 2nd ACM Symposium on Cloud Computing, SOCC 2011, pp. 5:1–5:14. ACM, New York (2011)
34. Sutton, R.S., Barto, A.G.: Reinforcement Learning: An Introduction, vol. 1. MIT Press, Cambridge (1998)

35. Tighe, M., Keller, G., Bauer, M., Lutfiyya, H.: DCSim: a data centre simulation tool for evaluating dynamic virtualized resource management. In: Network and Service Management (CNSM), 2012 8th International Conference and 2012 Workshop on Systems Virtualization Management (SVM), pp. 385–392 (2012)
36. Tseng, F.H., Wang, X., Chou, L.D., Chao, H.C., Leung, V.C.M.: Dynamic resource prediction and allocation for cloud data center using the multiobjective genetic algorithm. IEEE Syst. J. **12**(2), 1688–1699 (2018). https://doi.org/10.1109/JSYST.2017.2722476
37. Wang, J.V., Ganganath, N., Cheng, C.T., Tse, C.K.: Bio-inspired heuristics for VM consolidation in cloud data centers. IEEE Syst. J. **14**(1), 152–163 (2020). https://doi.org/10.1109/JSYST.2019.2900671
38. Watkins, C.J.C.H.: Learning from delayed rewards. Ph.D. thesis (1989)
39. Yadav, R., Zhang, W., Li, K., Liu, C., Shafiq, M., Karn, N.K.: An adaptive heuristic for managing energy consumption and overloaded hosts in a cloud data center. Wireless Netw. **26**(3), 1905–1919 (2018). https://doi.org/10.1007/s11276-018-1874-1

Secure Partitioning of Composite Cloud Applications

Alessandro Bocci[1(✉)], Roberto Guanciale[2], Stefano Forti[1], Gian-Luigi Ferrari[1], and Antonio Brogi[1]

[1] University of Pisa, Pisa, Italy
alessandro.bocci@phd.unipi.it,
{stefano.forti,gian-luigi.ferrari,antonio.brogi}@unipi.it
[2] KTH Royal Institute of Technology, Stockholm, Sweden
robertog@kth.se

Abstract. The security of Cloud applications is always a major concern for application developers and operators. Protecting their users' data confidentiality requires methods to avoid leakage from vulnerable software and unreliable cloud providers. Recently, hardware-based technologies emerged in the Cloud setting to isolate applications from the privileged access of cloud providers. One of those technologies is the Separation Kernel which aims at isolating safely the software components of applications. In this article, we propose a declarative methodology supported by a running prototype to determine the partitioning of a Cloud multi-component application in order to allow its placement on a Separation Kernel. We employ information-flow security techniques to determine how to partition the application, and showcase the methodology and prototype over a motivating scenario from an IoT application deployed to a central Cloud.

Keywords: Data Confidentiality · Separation Kernel · Information-flow Security

1 Introduction

The security aspects of Cloud Computing represent a major concern of both fundamental research and development, aiming at protecting data confidentiality and integrity of the applications running on the Cloud [21,28]. Some of those applications are composed of large codebases that rely on third-party software subject to frequent updates or short time-to-market. This makes it difficult to verify or certificate the security assurances of the released software, also exposing it to bugs that lead to exploitable vulnerabilities. Moreover, application operators exploiting the Cloud rely on cloud providers. Cloud providers deliver hardware and software infrastructure capabilities maintaining high privileges on the access to the infrastructure [8]. From the data security point of view, cloud providers cannot be considered fully reliable, e.g. a malicious insider could abuse its access rights to steal secret information [29].

© IFIP International Federation for Information Processing 2022
Published by Springer Nature Switzerland AG 2022
F. Montesi et al. (Eds.): ESOCC 2022, LNCS 13226, pp. 47–64, 2022.
https://doi.org/10.1007/978-3-031-04718-3_3

To protect applications data we consider the following scenario to place a multi-component application on the Cloud. On one hand, we want to isolate the components of an application in order to avoid leak of sensitive data by exploiting vulnerabilities of some components. On the other, we want to prevent access to the data of the application by unreliable cloud providers. To fulfill those requirements, application developers can exploit Trusted Execution Environments (TEEs) [1,2,7] to isolate the components of applications in *domains* allowing the data flow only using explicit communication channels and to elude the privileges of the hardware platform providers. TEEs provide in the Cloud the same memory and register isolation that is given by the Separation Kernel (SK) technology [23] In order to use these technologies, developers must decide which components should be grouped in the same domain, i.e. how to find a *partitioning* of the application to avoid data leaks. Given that the problem of how to partition an application is not dependent on the hardware that isolates the domains, in the rest of our discussion we refer to SKs as the supporting technology that comprehends TEEs and other similar technologies.

In this article, we tackle the partitioning problem employing information-flow security [24] methodologies (*i*) to understand whether the software components leak sensitive data outside the SK and (*ii*) to partition the application in order to avoid data leaks between components hosted on the same SK domain. We call *partitionable* those applications that do not leak data outside the SK, and we aim at finding a *minimal eligible partitioning* of such applications, namely a partitioning with the minimum number of domains that avoid data leaks.

Our contribution consists of:

(*a*) The definition of a declarative model to represent a multi-component application exploiting information-flow security to discriminate data confidentiality and to check whether the components manage their data without leaks,

(*b*) The (formal) definition of partitionable application and of the eligible partitioning problem, and

(*c*) A prototype of the above, SKnife[1], implemented in Prolog, to determine the minimal eligible partitioning of a partitionable application and an extension of the prototype capable of determining relaxed constraints of a non-partitionable application in order to be able to find the eligible partitioning.

The rest of this article is organised as follows. After giving background information and describing our motivating example (Sect. 2), we illustrate SKnife methodology and implementation (Sect. 3), which is then used to solve and discuss the motivating example (Sect. 4). After discussing some closely related work (Sect. 5), we conclude by pointing to some directions for future work (Sect. 6).

2   Background and Motivating Example

In this section, we first introduce basic notions behind the methodologies employed in our work and our motivating example.

---

[1] Open-sourced and freely available at: https://github.com/di-unipi-socc/sk.

2.1   Background

Scenario. We consider the public Cloud setting, where the cloud providers deliver hardware and software infrastructure to their customers. The applications are multi-components. Each software component of the application has a set of security-relevant characteristics, properties or software dependencies of the component, e.g. the use of a non verified third-party library. Those characteristics determine the degree of trust of a component in order to establish if the component can manage its data without leaks. The usage of software with a low degree of trust can lead to attacks that compromise the confidentiality of the data of an application. Hence, application developers need mechanisms (i) to identify how reliable software manage sensitive data, and (ii) to securely isolate components in order to avoid data leaks from unreliable software and (iii) to be protected by unreliable cloud providers.

Separation Kernels. An SK is a security kernel that creates an environment that is indistinguishable from a distributed system, where information can only flow from one isolated machine to another along explicit communication channels [23]. SKs are hardware or software mechanisms that partition available resources in isolated *domains* (or partitions), mediate the information flow between them, and protect all the resources from unauthorized accesses. In the Cloud setting, hardware-based technologies (TEEs) [1, 2, 7] are emerging to allow cloud providers customers to create isolated memory domains for code and data, which are also not accessible by the privileged software that is controlled by the cloud provider. Our approach is focused on the data separation given by SKs, we do not consider other sophisticated mechanisms offered, like the separation of resources and the timed scheduling of domains.

Information-Flow Security. In information-flow security, labels are assigned to variables of a program to follow its data flow in order to verify desired properties (e.g. non-interference [25]) and avoid covert channels. Labels are ordered in a security lattice to represent the relation of the labels from the highest ones (e.g. top secret) to the lowest ones (e.g. public data). Our goal is to prevent that data with a certain label (e.g. high) do not reach an external component that has a lower label (e.g. low). A violation of this security property indicates a data leakage.

Threat Model. Our goal is to protect the *data confidentiality* of multi-component Cloud applications. Vulnerable software components can be attacked by external attackers and by unreliable cloud providers that can exploit their superuser privileges on the infrastructure. Application developers are assumed trusted, the information they give about the application to protect is considered reliable. Our Trusted Computing Base (TCB) leverages on the SK technology to isolate the software components of the application in separate domains, guaranteeing that the information flows only along the explicit communication lines given by the application developers and avoiding other side channels. This model is consistent with threat model of several Trusted Execution Environments (e.g. [26]).

2.2   Motivating Example

We consider a Cloud centralised Internet of Things (IoT) system that collects data sampled by the sensors and send to the Cloud application, where data is stored and used to decide which commands to issue to the actuators. The users of this application can make requests on the status of the devices and can configure remotely the application. Nowadays, those kinds of applications are well established in the home automation field [5], services-devices composition [6] and platforms offered by Cloud providers [3,4].

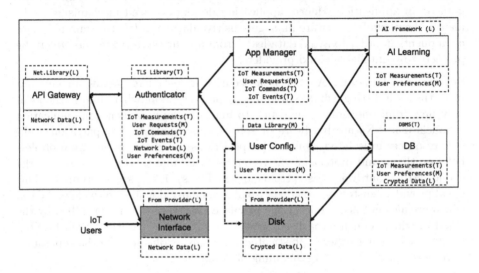

Fig. 1. Application architecture.

The architecture of the example application is depicted in Fig. 1. We consider six software components and two hardware components – depicted in grey – that are used by the application.

All the inbound communication passes through the `Network Interface` and is received by the `API Gateway`. `Authenticator` decrypts and authenticates the inbound data and forwards it to the intended recipient. Application users can send `General requests` and `configuration requests`. The former are requests of explicit actuation or data previously sampled and are delivered to the `App Manager`, which is the main component of the application that implement the business logic. The latter are requests of reading or updating the current application configuration and are delivered to the `User Configuration` component, which manages the configuration of the application. The IoT devices send either sampled data or events, which are dispatched to the `App Manager` component. The outbound communication consists of responses to the users based on their requests or IoT commands from the `App Manager` toward the IoT devices. To store the relevant data of the application – `IoT Measurement` and

User Preferences – the application relies on the component DB, a database that is the only one connected to the Disk. Finally, AI Learning is a machine learning module that uses IoT Measurement and User Preferences to perform predictions and support the decision making of the App Manager.

Each component has explicit links to other components, its own data – depicted in the lower boxes of the components –, and its relevant characteristics – depicted in the upper boxes of the components. For instance the component AI Learning has data IoT Measurement and User Preference, its relevant characteristic is AI Framework and it is linked to App Manager and User Configuration. The characteristics are properties, third-party libraries etc., all things that impact on the *trust* of the components. For instance, the Disk is owned by the Cloud provider that in our setting make the component unreliable. The measure of the trust level of components is mandatory to determine if they can manage their data in order to avoid leaks. For instance, the API Gateway must be able to manage its data to avoid the leak of such data toward the Network interface. The dotted arrow between User Config and Disk represent a link consisting of an alteration of the application architecture. Figure 1 represents two different application architectures with only that link as a difference. The base application – identified as iotApp1 – does not have the dotted link. The modified application – identified as iotApp2 – has the dotted link. We will use those two slightly different architectures in Sect. 4 when discussing the partitioning of the two applications.

This application results in a large codebase, which includes the operating system, communication stacks, AI frameworks, etc. It may also require frequent updates or short time-to-market. These factors make it hard to verify or certificate the security of the released software. Here, we propose to assign labels to the relevant characteristics of the application to determine the level of trust of software components. We also use the labels for the data of the application in order to establish a direct relationship between data and the trust of the software components. Here we adopt the security lattice of Fig. 2, modelling the labels pertaining to certain sensitive data from top (i.e. secret) to low (i.e. public), and trusted characteristics from top (i.e. highest trust) to low (i.e. not reliable). The labelling is represented in Fig. 1 by the letters between brackets placed near the data and characteristic names, where L stands for low, M stands for medium, and T stands for top.

A component having characteristics considered unreliable by the application developer is not able to manage secret data. This could cause a leak of its data toward the directly connected components or toward the software components hosted in the same isolation environment, i.e. container, virtual machine, SK domains. For instance, if the

Fig. 2. Example security lattice.

DBMS used by DB is not reliable – either because it is malicious or because it has vulnerabilities – the data of DB can leak toward the Disk, component owned by the Cloud Provider. Furthermore, if DB is isolated in the same SK domain of API Gateway (assuming a unreliable Net Library), the leak of data could flow from the DB to the Network Interface through the API Gateway.

We emphasise again that we aim at protecting data confidentiality of applications placed on the Cloud finding *eligible partitionings*, i.e. grouping the software components in non-empty subsets that allow placing the application in SK domains in such a way that the data and trust of the components are homogeneous in every domain, avoiding that less trusted components share the environment with components that manage sensitive data. For instance, we already discussed that AI Framework is a library of AI Learning considered not reliable, it may contain malicious code or its vulnerabilities may be exploited by an external attacker. Placing all the software components in the same environment (e.g. domain or virtual machine) exposes the data of the application to be read by AI Framework and sent outside the environment. Partitioning the application components to isolate their data and exploiting SKs isolation mitigates those kinds of threats.

Moreover, we want to reduce the number of domains used by the eligible partitioning to reduce the SK overhead that can heavily impact the application performance. For example, switching domain during the execution has a cost in terms of time that is influenced by the sanitising of used resources and by the domains scheduling algorithm of the SK. This kind of situation discourages the creation of a high number of domains. For this reason, we aim at finding the *minimal partitioning*, the eligible partitioning that creates the lowest number of domains.

3   Methodology and Prototype

This section describes the methodology which allows us to determine an *eligible partitioning* of an application onto an SK. We also discuss the Prolog[2] prototype SKnife supported by the methodology through simple examples excerpted from Sect. 2.2.

3.1   Modelling Applications and Labelling

Application developers model their application as in

```
application(AppId, ListOfHardware, ListOfSoftware).
```

where AppId is the application identifier, ListOfHardware is the list of hardware components interacting with the application, and ListOfSoftware is the list of software components to place on the SK.

Example. The iotApp1 application of our motivating example is declared as

---

[2] A Prolog program is a finite set of *clauses* of the form: a :- b1,...,bn. stating that a holds when b1 ∧ ⋯ ∧ bn holds, where n ≥ 0 and a, b1, ..., bn are atomic literals. Clauses with empty condition are also called *facts*. Prolog variables begin with upper-case letters, lists are denoted by square brackets, and negation by \+.

```
application(iotApp1, [network, disk],[userConfig, appManager,
            authenticator, aiLearning, apiGateway, db]).
```

Software and hardware components are declared as in

```
software(SwId, ListOfData, ListOfCharacteristics, [LinkedHW, LinkedSW] ).
hardware(HwId, ListOfData, ListOfCharacteristics, [LinkedHW, LinkedSW]).
```

where `SwId` and `HwId` are the unique identifiers of each component, `ListOfData` is the list of names of the data managed by the component, `ListOfCharacteristics` is the list of names of the component characteristics, `LinkedHW` is the list of linked hardware components and `LinkedSW` is the list of linked software components.

Example. The `db` and `disk` components are declared as

```
software(db, [iotMeasurements, userPreferences, cryptedData],
          [dbms], ([disk],[userConfig, managementLogic])).
hardware(disk, [cryptedData], [fromProvider],([],[db])).
```

Application developers must also declare a security lattice formed by ordered labels and they have to label the relevant data of the application and the relevant characteristics of the components. The higher is the label of data, the higher is the secrecy of the data. Similarly, the higher is the label of a characteristic, the higher is the trust of the characteristic. We call the labels assigned to data *secrecy labels* and the labels assigned to characteristics *trust labels*.

Every data and characteristic can be labelled using

```
tag(Name, Label).
```

where `Name` is the name of the data or characteristic to be labelled and `Label` is the assigned label. Obviously, the labels must be part of the lattice.

Example. The security lattice of Fig. 2 and the label of the data and the characteristics of the `Disk` are declared as

```
tag(cryptedData, low).
tag(fromProvider, low).
```

which represents `cryptedData` data with `low` secrecy label and `fromProvider` characteristic with `low` trust label.

3.2   Eligible Partitioning

Our methodology and SKnife as well assign to every component a pair of labels, one indicating its secrecy level and one indicating its trust level. A component is *trusted* if its trust label is greater or equal[3] than its secrecy label, otherwise, it is considered *untrusted*. A trusted component is able to manage its data without the risk of leaking them. The labelling of a component is performed by the predicate `labelC/3` of Fig. 3, using the lists of data and characteristics of the component. The secrecy label is determined by the highest label of its data in order to consider the most critical data managed by the component. The trust label is determined by the lowest label of its characteristics because the worst characteristic could compromise the trust of the component, e.g. a component using a simple logging library and a certified encryption software could be endangered by a bug in the former one. A component without relevant characteristics is considered reliable and its trust label is the highest one of the security lattice. We choose this level of granularity (i.e., the developer labels data and characteristics instead of directly labeling the components) to have a better insight of the application and to allow advanced features as the one that will be described in Sect. 3.3.

```
1   labelC(Data, Characteristics, (MaxType,CharactSecType)):-
2       dataLabel(Data,Labels),
3       highestType(Labels,MaxType),
4       characteristicsLabel(Characteristics, ListOfCharactTypes),
5       lowestType(ListOfCharactTypes, CharactSecType).
```

Fig. 3. The `labelC/3` predicate.

Untrusted components can leak their data to directly linked components. If such components have a trust label lower than the leaked data they can propagate the leakage through their links. If such data reach a hardware component, then an *external leak* occurs. An external leak is a path from an untrusted software component to a hardware component where all the components of the path have the trust label lower than the secrecy label of the first software component of the path. The presence of such paths indicates the potential for a data leakage from an untrusted component toward the outside of the SK that is not avoidable by the partitioning.

We say that an application is called *partitionable* is there is no leakage outside the SK: i.e., all its hardware components are trusted and all its untrusted software components do not have an external leak of data.

The predicate `hardwareOk/1` of Fig. 4 checks that all the hardware components of the application are trusted, which avoids hardware attacks that cannot be countered by the SK partitioning. The predicate recursively scans the list of hardware components to check their labelling. Initially, information of a single component is retrieved (line 2), then the labelling of the hardware component is determined (line 3). The predicate checks for the component trustability (line

---

[3] All the comparisons between labels are based on the ordering of the security lattice.

4), where `gte/2` checks if the trust is greater or equal than the secrecy. Finally, `hardwareOk/1` recurs on the rest of the list (line 5) until it is empty (line 6).

```
1   hardwareOK([H|Hs]) :-
2       hardware(H, Data, Characteristics,_),
3       labelC(Data, Characteristics, (TData,TChar)),
4       gte(TChar,TData),
5       hardwareOK(Hs).
6   hardwareOK([]).
```

Fig. 4. The `hardwareOk/1` predicate.

The predicate `softwareOk/1` of Fig. 5 checks that no software components (line 2) that is untrusted (line 3) has an external leak toward an untrusted hardware component (line 4).

```
1   softwareOk(LabelledSoftware):-
2       \+ (member((Sw,TData,TChar), LabelledSoftware),
3           lt(TChar,TData),
4           externalLeak([Sw], [] ,TData, LabelledSoftware)).
```

Fig. 5. The `softwareOk/1` predicate.

The software components of a partitionable application can be split and placed on SK domains. A domain is a triple (`DTData`, `DTChar`, `HostedSw`) where `DTData` is the secrecy label of the domain, `DTChar` is the trust label of the domain, and `HostedSw` is the list of the software components hosted by the domain. Inside a domain, software components share the same environment. To avoid placing components in an environment containing data that they are not able to manage, a domain must be *data consistent*:

$$\forall \texttt{software(Sw, Data,Characteristics,\_)} \in \texttt{HostedSw} :$$
$$\texttt{labelC(Data, Characteristics,(CTData,\_))} \rightarrow \texttt{PTData} = \texttt{CTData}$$

meaning that in a domain there is no software component with a secrecy label different from the domain secrecy label, i.e. all the software components hosted by a domain have the same secrecy label of the domain. This property avoids that a software component is placed in a domain that contains data more sensitive than the ones the component is supposed to deal with.

Another aspect to consider is that untrusted components bring out the risk to leak sensitive data to other components of the domain or to linked components outside the domain. In order to isolate such components, domains must be *reliable*:

∀software(Sw, Data,Characteristics,_) ∈ HostedSw :

        labelC(Data, Characteristics,(CTData,CTChar)) → CTData ≥ CTChar

∨

∀software(Sw, Data,Characteristics,_) ∈ HostedSw :

        labelC(Data, Characteristics,(CTData,CTChar)) → CTChar = PTChar

meaning that all the software components of a domain are either trusted or have the same trust label of the domain. Domains hosting only trustable software components are considered secure from data leaks. Every component can manage its data and can exchange it outside the domain without risk of leaks, according to the trust assigned by the developer. Untrusted components must be isolated strongly, they can share a domain only with other untrusted components having the same trust label, in order to have a homogeneous level of trust inside the domain and mitigate the danger of data leak.

Eligible partitionings split a partitionable applications into a set of data consistent and reliable domains. The top-level sKnife/2 (Fig. 6) finds the eligible partitioning of a partitionable application. After retrieving the application information (line 2), it basically performs two main steps, first it checks whether the application is partitionable (lines 3–5) and second it creates the set of data consistent and reliable domains splitting the software component across them (line 6), starting from en empty partitioning ([] of line 6).

The partitioning/3 predicate is listed in Fig. 7 and it has the task to split labelled software components placing them in data consistent and reliable domains. The predicate recursively scans the list of labelled software components (first argument) to place every component starting from a partitioning (second argument) that will be updated in the resulting partitioning (third argument). The domains of the resulting partitioning are data consistent and reliable by construction. Every software component is placed in a domain with the same secrecy label to satisfy the data consistency of the domain. Trusted components are placed together in domains with the trust label named safe, indicating that all the hosted components are trusted. Untrusted components are placed in the domain with the same trust label, in order to create reliable domains. If the domain needed by a component is not in the starting partitioning, it is created with correct labels and added to the partitioning. partitioning/3 has two main clauses (lines 1 and 6) plus the empty software list case that leaves the partitioning unmodified (line 11). The first case describes the situation in which a

```
1   sKnife(AppId, EligiblePartitioning) :-
2       application(AppId, Hardware, Software),
3       hardwareOK(Hardware),
4       softwareLabel(Software, LabelledSoftware),
5       softwareOk(LabelledSoftware),
6       partitioning(LabelledSoftware, [], EligibleParitioning).
```

Fig. 6. The sKnife/2 predicate.

```
1    partitioning([(S,TData,TChar)|Ss], Partitioning, NewPartitioning) :-
2        partitionCharLabel(TChar,TData,TCD),
3        select( ((TData,TCD), Ds), Partitioning, TmpPartitioning),
4        DNew = ( (TData,TCD), [S|Ds]),
5        partitioning(Ss, [DNew|TmpPartitioning], NewPartitioning).
6    partitioning([(S,TData,TChar)|Ss], Partitioning, NewPartitioning) :-
7        partitionCharLabel(TChar,TData,TCD),
8        \+ member( ((TData,TCD), _), Partitioning),
9        DNew = ( (TData,TCD), [S]),
10       partitioning(Ss, [DNew|Partitioning], NewPartitioning).
11   partitioning([],P,P).
```

Fig. 7. The partitioning/3 predicate.

software element can be placed on a domain already created. After determining the labelling of the hosting domain (line 2), the library predicate select/3 checks if such domain is already created in the partitioning (line 3) and extract it. Then, an updated domain is created by adding the current software component (line 4). Finally, partitioning/3 recurs on the rest of the software list giving as starting partitioning the old partitioning with the updated domain ([DNew|TmpPartitioning] of line 5).

The second clause of the predicate (line 6) describes the situation in which the domain that has to host the software component is not already in the input partitioning. The initial step to determine the hosting domain labelling is the same as the previous clause (line 7). Then, there is an explicit check that such domain is not already in the partitioning (line 8). At this point, the new domain is created (line 9) and it is included in the partitioning during the recursive call ([DNew | Partitioning] of line 10).

As mentioned in Sect. 2.2 it is important to reduce the number of domains of a partitioning as much as possible. We emphasise that SKnife main predicate outputs as unique solution the minimal eligible partitioning of the application, if it exists[4].

3.3   Labelling Suggestions

Not all the existing applications are partitionable, precluding the possibility to find an eligible partitioning. To assist application developers in those situations we added the feature to suggest *relaxed labellings* on data or characteristics of the applications. Those suggestions reduce the secrecy or increase the trustability of components relaxing the labelling of an application in order to find an eligible partitioning. This feature is intended to help the review of an applica-

---

[4] The extended version of this article with full proofs and other aspects is freely available at https://github.com/di-unipi-socc/sk/tree/main/Examples/CloudExample.

tion preventing the risk of leaking the confidentiality of data. Because of space limitations, we do not include code snippets of this version of SKnife[5].

The basic version of SKnife either finds the minimal partitioning or fails if there is a risk of data leak given by untrusted components. To support the suggestions feature, we suitably modified SKnife to individuate the source of a failure and to retry the partitioning after relaxing the labelling of such a source.

As aforementioned, the predicates that check if an application is partitionable are hardwareOk/1 and softwareOk/1. Those predicates are modified in order to return every single component responsible for a failure when the application is not partitionable. Then, the labelling of those components are *relaxed*, i.e. the data labels are decreased or the characteristics labels are increased. After that, the application is labelled with the relaxed labels and a new search for an eligible partitioning of the application starts. This retry mechanism is repeated until both the check predicates do not find a failure. The search eventually finds suggestions for an eligible partitioning. In the worst case scenario, the data labels will be relaxed to the lowest label of the lattice or the characteristics label will be relaxed to the highest label of the lattice.

The main predicate of the refinement of SKnife is sKnife/3. It has as the first argument the application identifier, as in the base version. The second argument is the list of relaxed labelling, pairs of data/characteristics names and the new relaxed label. The third argument is the eligible partitioning found with the relaxed labelling. Note that this predicate does not compute a unique solution. Indeed, for every query different relaxed labelling with the relative eligible partitioning are computed. This allows SKnife to give to the developer different suggestions.

4   Motivating Example Revisited

In this section, we will solve the partitioning problem of the architecture iotApp1 of the motivation example[6] of Sect. 2.2 given a suitable set of labels for every data and characteristic. Then, we will consider the slightly different iotApp2 architecture showing that it is not partitionable and we will apply the *relaxed labelling* feature of SKnife. In both cases the application architecture, the (software and hardware) components and the security lattice can be expressed as per the modelling of Sect. 3. Data and characteristics are labelled as indicated by the letters between brackets in Fig. 1 using the tag/2 predicate.

4.1   Finding the Minimal Partitioning

To find the minimal partitioning of iotApp1 we can simply query the sKnife/2 predicate as sKnife(iotApp1, Partitioning). Initially, SKnife labels all the

---

[5] Full code of the prototype extension at https://github.com/di-unipi-socc/sk/blob/main/Examples/CloudExample/skplacerRecommend.pl.

[6] Full example code at https://github.com/di-unipi-socc/sk/tree/main/Examples/CloudExample.

application components as depicted in Fig. 8, where is assigned a pair of label for each component, one for data and one for characteristics. For instance, App Manager is labelled top for its data (the T above the component) and top for its characteristics (the T below the component). Then, SKnife checks if the application is partitionable. The application is partitionable because the hardware components manage only low data and do not exist a path from AI Learning (the only untrusted component) to the hardware components that can leak top or medium data.

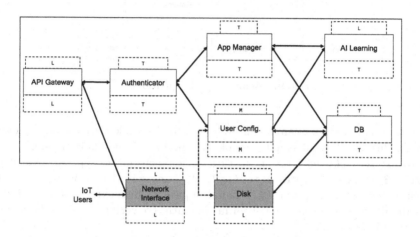

Fig. 8. Labelling of application components.

Figure 9 summarises the obtained result. The eligible partitioning is composed of 4 domains, 3 with trusted components (D1–D3) and 1 with an untrusted component (D4). It is a minimal partitioning because we have at least 3 software components with different secrecy labels and only 1 untrusted component and it is not possible to divide those components in less then 4 domains that are data consistent and reliable.

As aforementioned, SKnife outputs only a solution because the minimal eligible partitioning is unique, i.e. do not exist a partitioning of the application with a fewer or equal number of data consistent and reliable domains.

4.2 Relaxing the Labelling

To show the *relaxing labelling* feature we consider the architecture iotApp2 with the additional link between the User Configuration and the Disk. This link creates a path from the AI Learning to the Disk that can leak the top data IoT measurements and medium data User Preferences, making the application non partitionable. This happens because AI Learning is an untrusted component and can leak its data via its explicit links. The linked component User Configurations has trust label medium and it is not reliable to manage top

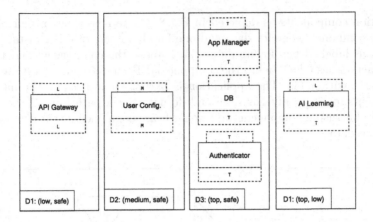

Fig. 9. Minimal eligible partitioning.

data, thus `IoT measurements` can be leaked to the `Disk` with the newly added link. In this situation, it is not possible to found an eligible partitioning.

To use the *relaxing labelling* feature on application `iotApp2` we can query `sKnife/3` predicate as `sKnife(iotApp2, S, Partitioning)`. As expected, the check performed by `softwareOk/2` founds a path with an external leak and individuate all the components involved in the path, triggering the retry behaviour explained in Sect. 3.3.

For the sake of clarity we show only the results to the query for the suggestion variable S, avoiding to display the eligible partitioning generated by applying the suggestions. The obtained results are

```
S=[(iotMeasurements,low),(userPreferences,low)]; S=(aiFramework,top);
S=(dataLibrary,top);                             S=(iotMeasurements,medium);
S=(fromProvider,top);                            S=(iotMeasurements,low).
```

For this specific situation, we can see that the solution is either reduce the security of `IoT Measurements` and `User Preferences` managed by `AI Learning`, cutting the path toward the `Disk`. When is analysed `AI Learning` the suggestion is to label `low` the data. When is analysed the second component of the path – `User Configuration` –, the suggestion is to reduce `IoT Measurements` to `medium`. Finally, when is analysed the last component of the path – `Disk` –, the suggestion is to reduce `IoT Measurements` to `low`. The alternatives increase the trust of each component of the path to cut the possible leak, increasing the characteristics `AI Framework`, `Data Library` and `From Provider` to `top`.

Those suggestions can support application developers to change the labelling if for instance the secrecy of `IoT Measurements` can be reduced. Otherwise, the suggestions could lead to changing the characteristics involved in the leak, for instance using a more reliable `Data library` for the component `User Configuration`.

Analysing each component of a path for every query can output overlapping solutions. For instance, `IoT Measurements` reduce to `low` appear two times. This can be avoided easily by searching all the suggestions at once and filtering the results.

5 Related Work

To the best of our knowledge, there are currently no proposals that employ information-flow security to place applications on SKs. Some approaches use information-flow security to address problems that are complementary to our techniques, for example checking the correct labelling of software or monitoring inputs and storage accesses by the applications. Elsayed and Zulkernine [15] propose a framework to deliver Information-Flow-Control-as-a-Service (IFCaaS) in order to protect confidentiality and integrity of the information flow in a SaaS application. The framework works as a trusted party that creates a call graph of an application from the source code and applies information-flow security based on dependence graphs to detect violation of the non-interference policy. At Function-as-a-Service (FaaS) level, Alpernas et al. [9] present an approach for dynamic Information-flow control monitoring the inputs of serverless functions to tag them with suitable security labels, in order to check access to data storage and communication channels to prevent leaks of data managed by the functions. Similarly, Datta et al. [14] propose to monitor serverless functions by starting to learn the information flow of an application, showing the detected flows to the developers and enforcing the selected ones. In the Cloud-IoT continuum scenario, our previous work [12] exploits information-flow security to place FaaS orchestrations on Fog infrastructures. Functions are labelled with security types according to input received and infrastructure nodes are labelled according to user-defined security policies. The placements are considered eligible if every node involved have the security type greater or equal than the security type of all the hosted serverless functions. Developers assign a level of trust to infrastructure providers that concurs to rank the eligible placements. Differently from SKnife, all those proposals but [15] consider the cloud provider reliable, conflicting with the threat model we introduced in Sect. 2. Recently, few proposals have leveraged on information flow analyses to enforce data security in cloud applications when the cloud provider is untrusted. For example, Oak et al. [22] have extended Java with information flow annotations that allow to verify if partitioning an application into components that run inside and outside a SGX enclave violate confidentiality security policies. In this proposal partitioning is decided by the programmer.

Other approaches aim at verifying the data separation and the data flow of SKs [10,13,18,27]. SKnife does not require special assumption on the SK and can be employed on all those SKs.

Similarly to SKnife, declarative techniques have been employed to resolve different Cloud-related problems. There are proposals to manage Cloud resources (e.g. [20]), to improve network usage (e.g. [19]), to assess the security and trust levels of different application placements (e.g. [16]), and to securely place VNF chains and steer traffic across them (e.g. [17]). To the best of our knowledge, there are currently no declarative proposals tackling our considered partitioning problem.

6   Concluding Remarks

This article introduced a declarative methodology and its prototype, SKnife, to protect the data confidentiality of Cloud applications from external attackers and unreliable cloud providers. Our approach exploits the Separation Kernel technology as Trusted Computing Base. It also employs information-flow security mechanisms to determine the eligible partitioning of a partitionable application to assist the placement of its software components in the Separation Kernel domains. To support the application developers, we extended SKnife with a feature that allows finding the eligible partitioning of non-partitionable applications relaxing the information-flow constraints given by application developers.

Our methodology requires manual labelling of data and characteristics of the application components. This limitation can be tackled using monitoring or automatic techniques to track information flow [11,14]. At the current stage, the flow of information is static, the data never change its labelling after the developer declaration. In our future work, we plan to support dynamic information flow, based on the application input and the relations between the software components. Moreover, we plan to support the labelling modification of an already partitioned application, correcting only the partitioning of the involved components, avoiding restarting from scratch the partitioning process. For instance, when a bug in a library used by a component is discovered, the label of the library can be reduced and the partitioning of the application can be changed accordingly. Another interesting direction is to extend our methodology to support data integrity. In addition to tackling all aforementioned points, we also plan to apply our methodology to different types of applications and to evaluate the effectiveness and scalability of our approach with experimental results. Finally, we plan to add a second feature to allow eligible partitioning of non-partitionable applications. We intend to use software engineering techniques to suggest modification of the application architecture in order to correct data leakage without changing the overall application behaviour.

References

1. AMD Secure Encrypted Virtualization (SEV). https://developer.amd.com/sev/. Accessed Nov 2021
2. Arm Confidential Compute Architecture (CCA). https://www.arm.com/why-arm/architecture/security-features/arm-confidential-compute-architecture. Accessed Nov 2021
3. AWS IoT Greengrass. https://aws.amazon.com/greengrass/. Accessed Nov 2021
4. Azure IoT Edge. https://azure.microsoft.com/services/iot-edge/. Accessed Nov 2021

5. Home Assistant. https://www.home-assistant.io/. Accessed Nov 2021
6. IFTTT. https://ifttt.com/. Accessed Nov 2021
7. Intel Trust Domain Extensions (TDX). https://www.intel.com/content/www/us/en/developer/articles/technical/intel-trust-domain-extensions.html. Accessed Nov 2021
8. Almorsy, M., Grundy, J.C., Müller, I.: An analysis of the cloud computing security problem. CoRR abs/1609.01107 (2016)
9. Alpernas, K., et al.: Secure serverless computing using dynamic information flow control. In: OOPSLA, vol. 2, pp. 1–26 (2018)
10. Andronick, J.: From a proven correct microkernel to trustworthy large systems. In: Beckert, B., Marché, C. (eds.) FoVeOOS 2010. LNCS, vol. 6528, pp. 1–9. Springer, Heidelberg (2011). https://doi.org/10.1007/978-3-642-18070-5_1
11. Bastys, I., Balliu, M., Sabelfeld, A.: If this then what? Controlling flows in IoT apps. In: ACM SIGSAC CCS 2018, pp. 1102–1119 (2018)
12. Bocci, A., Forti, S., Ferrari, G.L., Brogi, A.: Placing FaaS in the fog, securely. In: ITASEC 2021. CEUR Workshop Proceedings, vol. 2940, pp. 166–179 (2021)
13. Dam, M., Guanciale, R., Khakpour, N., Nemati, H., Schwarz, O.: Formal verification of information flow security for a simple arm-based separation kernel. In: ACM SIGSAC 2013, pp. 223–234. ACM (2013)
14. Datta, P., Kumar, P., Morris, T., Grace, M., Rahmati, A., Bates, A.: Valve: securing function workflows on serverless computing platforms. In: WWW, pp. 939–950 (2020)
15. Elsayed, M., Zulkernine, M.: IFCaaS: information flow control as a service for cloud security. In: ARES 2016, pp. 211–216. IEEE Computer Society (2016)
16. Forti, S., Ferrari, G.L., Brogi, A.: Secure cloud-edge deployments, with trust. Future Gener. Comput. Syst. **102**, 775–788 (2020)
17. Forti, S., Paganelli, F., Brogi, A.: Probabilistic QoS-aware placement of VNF chains at the edge. Theory Pract. Logic Program. **22**(1), 1–36 (2022)
18. Heitmeyer, C.L., Archer, M., Leonard, E.I., McLean, J.D.: Formal specification and verification of data separation in a separation kernel for an embedded system. In: ACMCCS 2006, pp. 346–355. ACM (2006)
19. Hinrichs, T.L., Gude, N.S., Casado, M., Mitchell, J.C., Shenker, S.: Practical declarative network management. In: WREN, pp. 1–10 (2009)
20. Kadioglu, S., Colena, M., Sebbah, S.: Heterogeneous resource allocation in Cloud Management. In: NCA 2016, pp. 35–38 (2016)
21. Kaufman, L.M.: Data security in the world of cloud computing. IEEE Secur. Priv. **7**(4), 61–64 (2009)
22. Oak, A., Ahmadian, A.M., Balliu, M., Salvaneschi, G.: Language support for secure software development with enclaves. In: IEEE Computer Security Foundations Symposium (CSF 2021) (2021)
23. Rushby, J.M.: Design and verification of secure systems. In: Proceedings of the Eighth Symposium on Operating System Principles, SOSP 1981, pp. 12–21. ACM (1981)
24. Sabelfeld, A., Myers, A.C.: Language-based information-flow security. IEEE J. Sel. Areas Commun. **21**(1), 5–19 (2003)
25. Sabelfeld, A., Sands, D.: A per model of secure information flow in sequential programs. High. Order Symb. Comput. **14**(1), 59–91 (2001)
26. Sahita, R., et al.: Security analysis of confidential-compute instruction set architecture for virtualized workloads. In: SEED, pp. 121–131. IEEE (2021)

27. Sewell, T., Winwood, S., Gammie, P., Murray, T., Andronick, J., Klein, G.: seL4 enforces integrity. In: van Eekelen, M., Geuvers, H., Schmaltz, J., Wiedijk, F. (eds.) ITP 2011. LNCS, vol. 6898, pp. 325–340. Springer, Heidelberg (2011). https://doi.org/10.1007/978-3-642-22863-6_24
28. Shaikh, F.B., Haider, S.: Security threats in cloud computing. In: ICITST 2011, pp. 214–219. IEEE (2011)
29. Tianfield, H.: Security issues in cloud computing. In: IEEE SMC 2012, pp. 1082–1089 (2012)

A Decentralized Service Control Framework for Decentralized Applications in Cloud Environments

Bram Hoogenkamp, Siamak Farshidi[✉], Ruyue Xin, Zeshun Shi, Peng Chen, and Zhiming Zhao[✉]

Multiscale Networked Systems, University of Amsterdam, Amsterdam, The Netherlands
{s.farshidi,r.xin,z.shi2,p.chen,z.zhao}@uva.nl

Abstract. Effectively managing decentralized applications in cloud environments using a decentralized control paradigm is essential, as current cloud providers usually only offer a control interface for monitoring cloud infrastructures. This study proposes a decentralized service control framework for implementing the control across various organizations and coordinating collaboration among operators in a decentralized application. The proposed framework allows a consortium of organizations to control a shared distributed cloud infrastructure decentralized reliably. A consensus mechanism within the framework enables mutual coordination between the operators. This mechanism also uses an incentive protocol to enforce pro-active behavior and collaboration. We implement the framework with Hyperledger Fabric, and our experiments demonstrate its usability, reliability, and acceptable performance.

Keywords: decentralized control · decentralized applications · consensus mechanism · collaboration protocol

1 Introduction

Recently, decentralized applications (dApps) have been employed in various industrial sectors, such as car sharing [12], data management [2], and finance [17]. The enabling technologies for dApps, such as Blockchain-as-a-Service (BaaS), have been included in numerous public cloud providers as part of their service portfolio, e.g., in Azure and AWS [3]. BaaS provides dApps with elastic distributed cloud infrastructures and often is operated using consortium blockchains. Current cloud providers usually offer a control interface for monitoring the cloud infrastructure, which is only for individual cloud service levels but not sufficient for dApps deployed by a consortium of organizations across different providers. Moreover, for dApps in cloud environments, it is only possible to track a failing part of the system, but organizations have no collaborative way to control the different cloud infrastructures. It is essential to implement the control across these various organizations and collaborate to achieve

F. Montesi et al. (Eds.): ESOCC 2022, LNCS 13226, pp. 65–73, 2022.
https://doi.org/10.1007/978-3-031-04718-3_4

global control. Therefore, a collaborative, decentralized control system on cloud infrastructures for a dApp is needed. In this research, we mainly focus on the question: *how to effectively manage a dApp in cloud environments with a decentralized control paradigm?* To answer this main research question, we analyze the requirements for a dApp control framework and conclude that control architecture and governance architecture are responsible for meeting decentralized requirements. In addition, coordination of decentralized control actions, including significant aspects of the consensus between peers and how to incentive collaboration between different peers, need to be investigated [14,15].

2 Decentralized Service Control Framework

In the literature, a variety of frameworks [6,7,10] for assessing the quality of services offered by different software producing organizations has been introduced. However, a control framework requires a peer-to-peer (p2p) control architecture [1] and an on-chain governance architecture [11] to control shared cloud infrastructures and maintain a high Quality of Service (QoS) of a dApp. In addition, a collaborative and proactive network in the control framework is needed. This study introduces a decentralized service control framework (DSConf) and elaborates on its architecture and constituent components.

2.1 Architecture Design

Operator agent, decentralized control consensus, and dApp/service control agent are the main components of the DSConf (see Fig. 1). The operator agent represents the operator of each organization in a dApp network, and it invokes the control layers which define different decentralized control patterns within the decentralized service control agent. Multiple control layers can be considered in a control architecture [16]. The lower-level control layer directly controls infrastructures/devices. The higher-level control layer is comprised of proposals and followed by a reply to execute or not (remote operators service operation) [13]. We also sub-divided service invocations into two categories: local dApp service invocations and remote dApp service invocations. Local dApp service invocations are performed by local services and consist of two control patterns: 1) operations on local service invoked by a local operator; 2) operations on local service invoked by remote operators. The Infrastructure as Code (IaC) service is invoked by logic defined on-chain in the first control pattern. The operator can call a local service function, and the function invokes the IaC service, which changes the state of the concerned infrastructure. In the second control pattern, a remote operator can propose a local dApp service invocation to one of the participating operators in the network. Remote dApp service invocations are performed on remote services (e.g., AWS). There are also two remote control patterns: 1) operations on remote services invoked by a local operator; 2) operations on remote services. In the first control pattern, an operator invokes a remote service. The second control pattern is a proposal sent to a global operator to invoke a remote service. We provide a global coordination mechanism for decentralized control consensus to achieve on-chain governance in a p2p network. With the mechanism, an operator can vote on a particular proposal that affects the whole network. **Decentralized service control agent** - In the decentralized service control agent, the network operators can execute and propose different control patterns. The service operations can be invoked locally and remotely. This decentralized service control agent uses the Co-util protocol to incentivize operators to list/verify these service invocations and propose/execute them. **Local dApp service invocation**can be performed without a proposal to DSConf and can act quickly if the QoS declines and concerns the operator's part of the shared infrastructures. The operator can invoke local services that invoke the IaC service (scale VM, migrate services, etc.), which will change the state of the infrastructure. Local dApp service invocations by *remote operators* make use of a proposed mechanism. We suppose an operator from organization X detects a decline in the QoS of the dApp caused by the infrastructure that organization Y provided. In that case, the operator from organization X can propose specific local dApp service invocations to organization Y. The operator from organization Y can accept/decline this proposal. By accepting the proposal, the IaC service will be invoked by the on-chain logic of the local service. **Remote dApp service invocation** is a possibility that an operator performs a remote dApp service invocation. For example, a service invocation on the AWS platform is not implemented locally. After executing this service invocation, the operator can list the performed remote dApp service invocation. The remote dApp service invocation will be verifiable. The incentive for listing these invocations will be explained in Sect. 2.1. Remote dApp service invocations by remote operators make use of *remote operators (proposal)*. For instance, an operator from organization X can send a proposal to organization Y to perform a remote dApp service invocation. The operator replies to this request and performs the specific operational invocation on a remote service. This reply triggers the operational invocation to get automatically listed to be verified by another operator. The following types of the remote dApp service invocation by remote operators: *Propose* remote dApp service invocation. Define: proposal id, organization id that proposes, organization id proposed to, service operation, description, remote dApp service invocation bit (e.q. operator A proposes a remote dApp service invocation to operator B). *Reply* to a remote dApp service invocation proposal. Define: proposal id, reply (e.q. Operator B replies to the remote dApp service invocation proposal. On agreement, the proposal gets listed to be verified by another operator. Operator B's service invocation uses a different system (e.q. AWS dashboard)). *Verify* listed service invocation. The *collaboration protocol* supports the decentralized service control agent to create a collaborative p2p network of operators. Often peers in a network need an incentive to help others. Our framework implemented a protocol that lets operators gain voting power by helping others. Moreover, the voting power can be used in the global coordination mechanism. The collaboration protocol exists in two parts: DSConf introduces non-transferable tokens representing the network's voting power. The *non-transferable token* represents an operator's voting power within the network.

It can be used in the weighted voting of the global DSConf proposal mechanism. An operator receives an initial amount of non-transferable tokens by joining the network: I_{amount}. The *Co-Util protocol* is introduced to enforce the operators to collaborate by increasing the operator's utility when helping other operators instead of displaying selfish behavior [4]. The action operators can take and the corresponding pay-off. Following the pay-off matrix, operators get rewarded for proposing, invoking, and verifying service invocations: the different operational control patterns and the associated rewards/penalties.

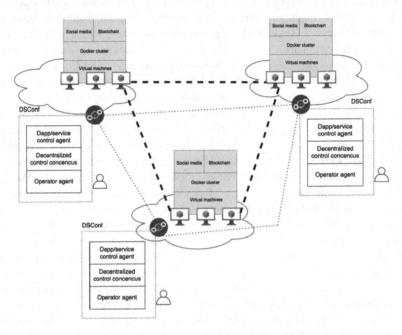

Fig. 1. Architecture design DSConf

2.2   Decentralized Control Consensus

An on-chain voting mechanism can enable the consortium to change/maintain the DSConf network. The global proposal module consists of four functions: *Create* a vote, which is an index, title, description, creator, timestamp, duration, list of operators that agree, list of operators that disagree, answer if is passed or did not pass. *Reply* on a vote, which is an index of the vote someone wants to reply to, the reply (agree/disagree). *Close* a vote, which is an index of the vote someone wants to close. *Get* all votes.

In addition, vote options could be about the following topics: 1) creating new control functions; 2) blocking operators; 3) onboarding operators.
Voting Incentivization Protocol. There is a need for a voting incentivization protocol to incentivize operators to behave pro-actively in these votes. The voting

mechanism will use non-transferable tokens that represent the voting power of an operator. This voting power can be used in global proposals. Every peer in the DSConf network will get an initial amount of I_{amount} by joining the network. The stakes will be evenly distributed in the initial state of the DSConf network [5,9]. A Proof of Stake(PoS) mechanism will be used to incentivize operators to vote on these proposals because choices often have to be made quickly. There has to be an incentive for the operators to reply as soon as possible. A debating period can be set for a vote in the voting process. When someone responds within the debating period, her new stake will be $C_{amount} + REWARD$. Where C_{amount} is the current amount of voting power the operator posses. If the participant of the DSConf did not manage to vote within this period, the penalty would be that they get slashed. This means that the new amount of their stake will be $C_{amount} - PENALTY$ [8]. *Development proposal.* The DSConf network could deploy new functionalities, update current functionalities, or change existing governance mechanisms. One of the participating organizations/operators can negotiate an off-chain deal to hire a developer. After that, the operator can vote to decide if the DSConf agrees with the proposal and the negotiated terms. If the DSConf agrees, everybody has to deposit the funds off-chain to the operator that arranged the proposal. Granted that everybody deposits, the operators confirm the proposal with the developer. *Block/unblock malicious operator.* A vote could be about blocking malicious operators. If the malicious activity is monitored, an operator can invoke a vote, report an operator, and describe the violation. If the vote passes, the operator is blocked for a certain amount of time. *On-boarding proposal.* The proposal could also be about onboarding an organization. There can be a vote to decide if a new organization can be added to the DSConf network.

3   Experiments

The purpose of our experiments is to verify the key performance indicators of the DSConf. These indicators are 1) usability, 2) reliability, 3) time-critical performance. The transactions to the DSConf chaincode contracts will be executed and captured in a shell environment. We observe the operator states as the output of the chaincode invocation for each control pattern.

Usability - In this section, the usability of DSConf is tested. We test the operational action contracts, and there are four control patterns and a voting mechanism that need to be tested. After every experiment of a control pattern, the ledger is re-initiated and the contracts redeployed, so the results are more straightforward to understand. *Local dApp service invocation by local operator,* in which the operator Org1MSP invokes a local service operation, and it does not need approval from others to invoke this operation. After executing the invocation functions, we can retrieve the different operators to see if the reward of $+2$ is assigned to Org1MSP. In Table 1, we can see that the reward is assigned correctly.

Table 1. Operators state with different control functions

Control pattern	OclToken			Reply
	Org1MSP	Org2MSP	Org3MSP	
Local-Local	202	200	200	–
Local-Remote	202	201	200	Agree
	199	200.5	200	Disagree
Remote-Local	201	202	200	–
Remote-Remote	201	200	200	Agree
	201	202	201	Disagree
Global	200	200	200	–

Reliability - The reliability of the DSConf network can be tested by experimenting with the disruption of the network. Experiments regarding the reliability of the service invocations are performed by executing the different functions implemented in the Global DSConf voting contract. Important to mention is the V_{min} variable that is set to 60. This means that 60% of the organization has to reply on a vote to pass. Org2MSP will be the organization that is offline in this experiment. Subsequently, Org1MSP will create a vote and immediately reply to this vote. After that, Org3MSP will reply and close the vote. The reliability results show that if a disturbance in the network arises, in this case, one organization node that is unreachable in a network of three organization nodes, the network still functions. The decentralized control functions in the network are still operational, and control invocations can still be proposed to the unreachable node. However, the unreachable node first has to be reachable again to invoke control actions.

Table 2. Time spend of service invocation

Execution time - Milliseconds(MS)			
Functions	Average (10x)	Fastest	Slowest
Action proposal	2.24	1.51	3.33
Execute action by proposal	16.31	10.73	29.83
Execute action without proposal	15.2516	10.48	25.12
List action	3.38	1.87	5.34
Reply proposal	16.18	14.21	20.11

Time Critical Performance. In the performance experiments, the execution time of the different functions is measured. These measurements of the DSConf are essential because of the time-critical nature of certain service invocations. The execution measurement is performed from the beginning of the chaincode call until the end of the function executions, returning the return value and execution time. Another critical aspect of the architecture is that functions within the DSConf network are sequential. We measure the execution performance of the chaincode functions. Every function is executed ten times to gather enough data.

We evaluate the performance of *service invocation* and the *global DSConf voting mechanism*. The ' Execute action' function is the most crucial function to measure execution time. This function has to perform time-critical operations on the concerned infrastructure.

Table 3. Time spend of voting mechanism

Execution time - Milliseconds(MS)			
Functions	Average(10x)	Fastest	Slowest
Create vote	2.66	1.24	5.18
Reply vote	3.06	2.39	4.94
Close vote	6.42	5.81	7.93

In these experiments, the execution time of the different functions was measured. The essential functions to measure were the local dApp service invocation functions. In Table 2, these functions take around 16ms to execute, which is within a second. However, the execution time does not include the invocation of the IaC service. The other DSConf functions lie within an execution time of 2 to 30 ms, also within a second. In Table 3, we can see that the execution time of each function in the voting mechanism is under 10 ms. So the overall performance of this experiment seems good.

4   Conclusion

In this research, we focus on how to effectively manage a dApp in cloud environments using a decentralized control paradigm. To conclude this question, we provide a review of the decentralized control framework at first. The review concludes that a p2p network and on-chain governance are essential for a decentralized control framework. In addition, there is a need for an incentive to enforce collaboration between operators in the p2p network.

To coordinate the decentralized control action within a p2p network and achieve on-chain governance, we provide a decentralized service control framework DSConf. In DSConf, a decentralized service control agent that uses a collaboration protocol to incentivize operators to collaborate is provided. In addition, a consensus voting mechanism enables mutual coordination between the operators in the DSConf network. This mechanism also uses an incentivization protocol to enforce pro-active behavior.

Acknowledgment. This work has been partially funded by the European Union's Horizon 2020 research and innovation programme by the ENVRI-FAIR (824068), BLUECLOUD (862409), and ARTICONF(825134) and by the LifeWatch ERIC.

References

1. Almasalma, H., Engels, J., Deconinck, G.: Peer-to-peer control of microgrids. In: 8th IEEE Benelux Young Researchers Symposium in Electrical Power Engineering (2016)
2. Bergers, J., Shi, Z., Korsmit, K., Zhao, Z.: Dwh-dim: a blockchain based decentralized integrity verification model for data warehouses. In: 2021 IEEE International Conference on Blockchain (Blockchain), pp. 221–228 (2021). https://doi.org/10.1109/Blockchain53845.2021.00037
3. Dhillon, V., Metcalf, D., Hooper, M.: Blockchain Enabled Applications. Apress, Berkeley (2017)
4. Domingo-Ferrer, J., Martínez, S., Sánchez, D., Soria-Comas, J.: Co-utility: self-enforcing protocols for the mutual benefit of participants. Eng. Appl. Artif. Intell. **59**, 148–158 (2017)
5. Fan, X., Chai, Q., Zhong, Z.: MULTAV: a multi-chain token backed voting framework for decentralized blockchain governance. In: Chen, Z., Cui, L., Palanisamy, B., Zhang, L.-J. (eds.) ICBC 2020. LNCS, vol. 12404, pp. 33–47. Springer, Cham (2020). https://doi.org/10.1007/978-3-030-59638-5_3
6. Farshidi, S., Jansen, S.: A decision support system for pattern-driven software architecture. In: Muccini, H., et al. (eds.) ECSA 2020. CCIS, vol. 1269, pp. 68–81. Springer, Cham (2020). https://doi.org/10.1007/978-3-030-59155-7_6
7. Farshidi, S., Jansen, S., Fortuin, S.: Model-driven development platform selection: four industry case studies. Softw. Syst. Model. **20**(5), 1525–1551 (2021). https://doi.org/10.1007/s10270-020-00855-w
8. Leonardos, S., Reijsbergen, D., Piliouras, G.: Weighted voting on the blockchain: improving consensus in proof of stake protocols. Int. J. Network Manage **30**(5), e2093 (2020)
9. Nguyen, C., Dinh Thai, H., Nguyen, D., Niyato, D., Nguyen, H., Dutkiewicz, E.: Proof-of-stake consensus mechanisms for future blockchain networks: fundamentals, applications and opportunities 1 (2019). https://doi.org/10.1109/ACCESS.2019.2925010
10. Poon, L., Farshidi, S., Li, N., Zhao, Z.: Unsupervised anomaly detection in data quality control. In: 2021 IEEE International Conference on Big Data (Big Data), pp. 2327–2336. IEEE (2021)
11. Reijers, W.: Now the code runs itself: on-chain and off-chain governance of blockchain technologies. Topoi **40**(4), 821–831, e2093 (2018). https://doi.org/10.1007/s11245-018-9626-5
12. Saurabh, N., et al.: The ARTICONF approach to decentralized car-sharing. blockchain: research and applications 1–37 (2021). https://doi.org/10.1016/j.bcra.2021.100013
13. Stanciu, A.: Blockchain based distributed control system for edge computing. In: 2017 21st International Conference on Control Systems and Computer Science (CSCS), pp. 667–671 (2017). https://doi.org/10.1109/CSCS.2017.102
14. Tran, H., Hitchens, M., Varadharajan, V., Watters, P.: A trust based access control framework for p2p file-sharing systems. In: Proceedings of the 38th Annual Hawaii International Conference on System Sciences, pp. 302c–302c. IEEE (2005)

15. Wang, Y., Nguyen, T.L., Xu, Y., Tran, Q.T., Caire, R.: Peer-to-peer control for networked microgrids: multi-layer and multi-agent architecture design. IEEE Trans. Smart Grid **11**(6), 4688–4699, e2093 (2020)
16. Wang, Y., Nguyen, T.L., Xu, Y., Tran, Q.T., Caire, R.: Peer-to-peer control for networked microgrids: multi-layer and multi-agent architecture design. **11**, 4688–4699 (2020). https://doi.org/10.1109/TSG.2020.3006883
17. Wu, K., Ma, Y., Huang, G., Liu, X.: A first look at blockchain-based decentralized applications. Practice and Experience, Software (2019)

Service Design and Development

A Systematic Comparison of IoT Middleware

Florian Held[(✉)], Philipp Schauz, and Jörg Domaschka

Institute of Information Resource Management, Ulm University, Ulm, Germany
{florian.held,philipp.schauz,joerg.domaschka}@uni-ulm.de

Abstract. The Internet of Things (IoT) is a constantly growing domain in information technology that involves various hardware and software layers and many different programming abstractions and paradigms. As such, a large number of IoT middleware systems has grown together with the IoT. Hence, selecting an IoT middleware is therefore a time-consuming task, if the goal is to achieve interoperability between all devices and retaining their functionality.

A systematics for classifying, comparing, and ranking various IoT middleware offerings reduces complexity in the selection process and provides insights regarding a feature-wise comparison. In this paper, we introduce such a systematics and apply it on a large set of open source middleware systems orientated towards IoT. Concerning the best overall ranking, *ThingsBoard* emerged as the candidate with the highest score.

Keywords: Internet of Things · Middleware · Evaluation · Ranking

1 Introduction

The *IoT* is semantically described as "A world-wide network of interconnected objects uniquely addressable, based on standard communication protocols" [7]. Therefore, it covers a wide field that includes private projects like Smart Home applications and large industrial projects with global reach. In all these cases, the main aspect is the communication of devices which are commonly labelled as things. These devices have many characteristics like heterogeneity, resource constraints and spontaneous interactions [11,15].

This led to middleware systems, which address the interaction between heterogeneous devices and communication forms by abstracting from available technologies. To achieve this, different integrated services for interconnection, device discovery, management of resources, data, events and device code are required [15].

As of today, only a combination of different middleware systems are able to handle all the requirements of the IoT [15]. So far, there are only attempts to achieve this by building a unified middleware solution from scratch [12]. This architectural approach takes a lot of effort and so far no satisfying solution has been created. This restriction implies that, based on the individual IoT use

© IFIP International Federation for Information Processing 2022
Published by Springer Nature Switzerland AG 2022
F. Montesi et al. (Eds.): ESOCC 2022, LNCS 13226, pp. 77–92, 2022.
https://doi.org/10.1007/978-3-031-04718-3_5

case, a proper middleware candidate must be chosen trying to fulfill most of the associated requirements. As there is a vast number (our investigation yielded 135) of IoT middleware systems available on the market, there is a need to first distill qualified candidates with moderate complexity. As will be shown and motivated, one of the exclusion criterion was a non open source model for a middleware. Second, there needs to be a formal mechanism enabling to map properties, i.e. features, of the remaining candidates to the requirements of the use case eventually giving the user the opportunity to make his final selection.

Therefore, our chosen approach is to investigate on already existing middleware by evaluating them feature-wise in a quantitative fashion. Eventually this leads to an absolute ordering in the case of considering and weighting all features and to a relative ordering if only certain features are taken into account. As was the given goal this provides opportunities and flexibility for selecting a middleware tailored to a special use case or when individual features play a significant role.

For this purpose, a system to select, compare, rank and evaluate middleware systems is required. To define this system, already existing evaluation approaches are taken as reference [3,11,13,15].

To investigate our system in practice, we applied it to a vast set of middleware systems, of which some were not considered yet in related work. In conclusion, the aim is to answer the following research questions:

- How can the approach be formalized with a sufficiently accurate mathematical model?
- Compared to previous evaluations, which new middleware systems are there and what capabilities do they offer?
- Can the approach be applied with moderate complexity to all findable middleware systems?

The reminder of this paper is structured as follows. Section 2 presents background information on *IoT* characteristics and associated middleware requirements. This is followed by a discussion on related work in Sect. 3. Section 4 covers our three-step methodology by first describing our middleware selection procedure, followed by the definition of a mathematical model to extract and quantify features. Eventually it is shown how the results of the last step can be utilized and evaluated. Section 5 applies the methodology and presents the results. In Sect. 6 we draw our conclusions.

2   Background

In this Section, we discuss general IoT characteristics and use the results as a foundation for defining requirements IoT middleware systems, respectively their offered services, should satisfy.

2.1 IoT Characteristics

Borgia [1] and Perera et al. [14] extract the following *IoT* characteristics relevant for middleware systems:

Scalability: As there are billions of devices and objects attributable to the IoT today, there need to be mechanisms able to manage and coordinate these vast numbers.

Heterogeneity: Besides quantity in horizontal dimension, there is also quantity in vertical dimension. This quantity can be described by heterogeneity of device architectures and communication technologies. Again, there need to be mechanisms considering and solving these issues.

Self-*: This characteristic encompasses concepts like self-configuration or self-organization. Precondition to manage the aforementioned large scales is the availability of automated mechanisms like self-discovering of entities and services or self-processing of Big Data.

Everything-as-a-Service: As the *IoT* does not only scale geographically but also in terms of domains (e.g. healthcare) and stakeholders (operators, developers, users, software entities), it needs to provide capabilities to satisfy the respective needs. A popular solution for this is to offer respective capabilities as services. For an operator this could mean, managing relevant resources in an Infrastructure-as-a-Service (IaaS) fashion.

Secure environment: Due to worldwide device distribution, heterogeneity and high amount of wireless communication, attack surfaces dramatically increase. For this reason, it is crucial that mechanisms to secure the IoT environment are employed.

2.2 IoT Middleware Requirements

IoT middleware systems are mostly deployed in an edge or fog environment [15]. The following general requirements can be attributed to them linked to the aforementioned characteristics:

Device Discovery: This addresses the problem of finding useful devices in order to accomplish a task [2]. Precondition for this is that the middleware is able to exploit different heterogeneous technologies of communication like Wi-Fi, Bluetooth or *MQTT*. This requirement is linked to the *Scalability*, *Heterogeneity* and *Self-* characteristics.

Resource Management: Generally, an *IoT* middleware should try to allocate resources fairly and provide the tools to monitor resource consumption [11, 15]. Moreover, it should offer basic resilience mechanisms. This requirement is linked to the *Self-* and *Everything-As-a-Service* characteristics.

Data Management: This refers to the requirement of the *IoT* middleware to store data and make it available to other devices. Additionally, it handles data compression and aggregation [11,15]. This requirement is linked to the *Self-*, *Everything-As-a-Service* and *Secure environment* characteristics.

Code Management: In general this requires the *IoT* middleware to deploy software changes to devices. This allows to reprogram a device and therefore improves maintenance [15]. This requirement is linked to the *Heterogeneity, Self-** and *Secure environment* characteristics.

3   Related Work

Razzaque et al. [15] start with a discussion on what fields are comprised by *IoT*. It then steps over to the concept of middleware systems and divides them in seven different design approaches and compares the 61 candidates. The comparison is based on specific characteristics of *IoT*. In the end it discusses challenges related to the different requirements that originate from the *IoT* characteristics. This work provides an overview of available middleware systems and is a reference to identify requirements and build a system to assess and evaluate middleware systems. Their approach is similar to ours taken. However, by just describing and not quantifying feature characteristics, a quantifiable comparison and ranking of middleware candidates is not possible. Moreover, some recently emerged and promising IoT middleware systems could not be taken into account in this work.

The work of Ngu et al. [13] focuses in the beginning on a case study to measure blood alcohol content with different sensors in *IoT*. Then it compares service-based, cloud-based and actor-based middleware systems. In the end it gives a summary of challenges and theoretical solutions for discovery and security cases. This reference provides insights into features of a domain specific middleware and helps to differentiate between more general features. In the paper, there is a summary of a small set of IoT middleware systems and associated provided functionalities (e.g. *Network Connectivity*). Compared to our approach, only a small set of systems is taken into account and just a description of the provided functionalities, respectively features, is given.

Cruz et al. [3] discuss different communication methods that are all relevant for the *IoT*. Then it splits different *IoT* middleware systems in categories. This is followed by a discussion of some examples. In the end it gives some new ideas on how to improve the security of *IoT* middleware systems. It is a relatively new paper that again describes functionalities of relevant *IoT* middleware systems however without quantification and comparison.

Marques et al. [10] compare different middleware systems and show which features they support. Furthermore, they look specifically at the healthcare field. There the different devices and protocols in use are shown. This reference provides an approach to compare protocols and gives insights on the healthcare domain. Their approach is similar to the proposed one, with the distinctions that only a small set, tailored to the healthcare domain, less features and no quantification is presented.

The work of Nastic et al. [12] focuses on middleware for *IoT* cloud systems. For this purpose it looks at a multitude of components in detail. They build a prototype that achieves high scalability and state that it should be relatively easy to extend it. This reference gives insights on the specific software components and services, a middleware could be created of. Furthermore, it gives a lot of information about cloud based middleware systems.

4 Methodology

In order to find a suitable way to answer our first research question, we use the following methodology. This methodology is derived from the approaches in similar works and tailored to the discussed requirements of *IoT* middleware systems. In particular, from related work we took into account the results from [3,10,13,15] for the chosen features and for the formal representation of feature-characteristics for considered features (cf. Sect. 4.2) we considered results from [15]. The new contributions of our approach are *first*, a formal model for quantifying IoT middleware systems feature-wise. *Second*, the presentation of evaluation possibilities for the results of the quantification. *Third* an initial preprocessing step to reduce the initial large pool of candidates to a feasible size able to be quantified feature-wise.

We start with the preprocessing step and outline how the initial pool of candidates can be found, followed by describing the steps that are taken to reduce the initial pool. Next, we present the formal model, describing how to quantify the remaining candidates feature-wise. Eventually we outline evaluation possibilities for the results of the previous step.

4.1 Middleware Selection Process (Preprocessing)

To find an initial pool of candidates, the first step is to get an efficient overview of relevant middleware systems. Therefore, a literature analysis is conducted. The focus is laid on papers that investigated multiple middleware systems in previous years. Afterwards, a more general search for publications referencing newly released middleware systems is made, that so far were not yet covered in papers analysing individual *IoT* middleware systems. Eventually, an investigation about software that offer similar services, e.g. *IoT* platforms with an integrated middleware part, is conducted.

The overall goal of the selection process is to find a set of relevant middleware systems from a pool of potential candidates with moderate expenditure. Therefore, the first goal is to efficiently reduce the possibly vast pool of candidates. This is done by defining simple exclusion criteria. The reason behind this is that the strict formal approach that a middleware can be excluded if another middleware can be found which is quantitatively better or equal in all considered aspects is not feasible as it requires in-depth knowledge about the middleware and possible use cases. Therefore, easy to apply and reasonable elimination criteria are chosen. As a boundary condition, we forced each elimination step to reduce the remaining pool's size by at least $\frac{1}{5}$ in every iteration step.

4.2 Feature Quantification Process

The previous process gives no information about a possible absolute or feature-wise ordering of the middleware systems. Therefore, the remaining candidates are scanned for implemented features that are in conjunction with the defined general IoT middleware requirements. This resulted in a set of considered features $\vec{x} \in X$, where $x_i \in X_i$ is the respective feature characteristic, of an inspected feature X_i. A feature characteristic is always mapped to at most 4 distinct symbol-values: $x_i \in \{s_{i,0}, s_{i,1}, s_{i,2}, s_{i,3}\}$. To quantify the feature characteristic, a single mapping function f is needed $f : X_i \mapsto \{0, 1, 2, 3\}$, where following conditions always hold for every feature X_i:

$$f(s_{i,0}) = 0 \tag{1}$$
$$f(s_{i,1}) = 1 \tag{2}$$
$$f(s_{i,2}) = 2 \tag{3}$$
$$f(s_{i,3}) = 3 \tag{4}$$

which maps the extracted feature characteristic to a corresponding numerical value. For illustration purpose, we look at the definition of a feature X_1

$$X_1 = \{\text{none, basic, advanced, custom}\} \tag{5}$$

then for the feature-characteristic x_1 holds:

$$x_1 \in \{none, basic, advanced, custom\} \tag{6}$$

and for the symbol-values of x_1:

$$f(\{none\}) = 0 \tag{7}$$
$$f(\{basic\}) = 1 \tag{8}$$
$$f(\{advanced\}) = 2 \tag{9}$$
$$f(\{custom\}) = 3 \tag{10}$$

Eventually this formalism allows to compare the middleware systems feature-wise.

4.3 Evaluation Process

The previous process in our approach builds the foundation for a flexible evaluation. If only a single feature is taken into account, a comparison and ranking without further effort can be conducted. However, if more than one feature is taken into account, one possibility is to define a score for the individual middleware systems by summing over weighted mapped feature characteristics as defined in the Quantification Process. This can be formalized as follows with N being the total number of features:

$$S_{k,\vec{\omega}}(\vec{x}) = \sum_{i \subseteq \{1..k\}} \omega_i f(x_i) \; ; \quad k \leq N \tag{11}$$

The values for the weight vector $\vec{\omega}$ entries are set to lower values if the feature appears to be less relevant for the final evaluation. Of course this is a subjective assumption and therefore needs to be justified for general use cases. If not directly specified at respective places, features x_i are assumed to have a weight $\omega_i = 1$. Other possible weights ω_i are $\frac{1}{2}$ and $\frac{1}{4}$. This allows for two decrease options for less relevant features and thus the ability to linearly scale results of the mapping function f.

5 Application of the Approach

We now apply the proposed methodology to IoT middleware systems that were traceable and attributable as of *June 2021*. In particular, the exclusion criteria in the *Selection Process*, the quantifiable features and mappings in the *Quantification Step* and the results in the *Evaluation Process* will be presented. As will be shown, due to our proposed approach, it was possible to derive quantifiable results for evaluation with moderate effort, yielding an answer for research question three.

5.1 Middleware Selection Process (Preprocessing)

As a starting point, middleware systems that were referenced in prior investigations [3,10–13,15] or that are popular for *IoT* applications were collected. This resulted in a collection of **135** *IoT* middleware systems. Compared to the 61 candidates investigated in [15], we were able to drastically increase the initial pool size and account for possible new functionality of the candidates.

Eliminate Middleware Systems not Being Open Sourced. A precondition for a better understanding of software architecture, implementation and features is that the code is open sourced. Furthermore, for reasoning in the *Feature Quantification* step, it is of great benefit, if all sources (code, documentation) are publicly available. So, in this step, middleware systems not fulfilling this criterion were excluded. A popular approach to share code is to publish it on GitHub, where most of the open sourced initial candidates could be found. Through this step, the middleware candidates could be reduced to **40**.

Eliminate Inactive Projects. As technological and conceptual changes happen steadily in the IoT, so is the job of an *IoT* middleware to rapidly adapt to those new realities. This means that middleware systems that do not adhere to this process should be neglectable in the mid-term.

Under this assumption, we excluded middleware systems from further investigation with no release in the year 2020 or later. Through this step, the middleware candidates could be reduced to **17**.

Eliminate by Application Domain and Production Readiness. This step eliminates middleware systems, if the application domain is too narrow or the middleware is not ready for production. To check if the application domain is too narrow its architecture is compared to the *IoT* middleware requirements in Sect. 2 and typical *IoT* domains (Industrial, Consumer and Home, Healthcare, Infrastructure, Transportation, Retail). To check if a middleware is ready for production, it needs to fulfill two conditions: all named requirements need to be addressed and continuous support should be available.

Under this assumption, we further excluded middleware systems and reduced the pool of candidates to **9**.

Eliminate Middleware with Low Popularity. The last elimination step is based on an analysis of the community and the precondition that the remaining middleware projects were all hosted on GitHub. For this purpose, the remaining middleware systems were sorted in decreasing order for both the parameters *watch* and *star*. Then, their average value for their ranking in both categories was calculated to get a final ordering. From this, the two worst performing middleware systems were excluded, as this fits the precondition of eliminating at least $\frac{1}{5}$ of the remaining candidates. At this point, the corner case of a popular middleware of the past could come to mind with a high star and watch number received years ago. The probability to make a flawed decision at this point was tried to keep at a minimum by a priori executing the *Inactive Projects* and *No Continuous Support* (cf. paragraph *Eliminate by Application Domain and Production Readiness*) elimination steps.

Through this, we reduced the pool of candidates to **7**.

Final Results of the Selection Process. With the help of our Selection Process, we were able to reduce the original pool of 135 candidates to 7, which is about 5% of the original population. This final number made a feasible investigation in the upcoming *Feature Quantification Process* possible. The remaining candidates after finalizing this step are listed in the following table (Table 1):

Table 1. Remaining middleware candidates after Selection Process

Name	Source Code URL
Eclipse Kapua	https://github.com/eclipse/kapua
Mainflux	https://github.com/mainflux
OpenRemote	https://github.com/openremote
SiteWhere	https://github.com/sitewhere
ThingsBoard	https://github.com/thingsboard
Fiware	https://github.com/Fiware
Node-RED	https://github.com/node-red

5.2 Feature Quantification Process

In the Quantification Process, the remaining candidates are rated feature-wise based on the methodology described in Sect. 4. As a basis to define relevant features served the results of Sect. 2, previous investigations on other middleware systems [3, 10, 13, 15] and common functionality patterns that emerged during the investigation. Summarized, our methodology will be applied to following features in this section:

- X_1 : Abstraction and Model Terminology
- X_2 : Connectivity
- X_3 : Deployment
- X_4 : Persistent Communication and Message Handling
- X_5 : Security
- X_6 : User Management - Authorization
- X_7 : Data and Action Processing
- X_8 : Resilience Mechanisms
- X_9 : Scaling Technologies
- X_{10}: Cloud Hosting Support
- X_{11}: Data Visualization
- X_{12}: Data Analytics
- X_{13}: License Model
- X_{14}: Scalability and Stability Performance

Abstraction and Model Terminology. The terminology used by the middleware systems is not always consistent, so an abstraction is required to compare the capabilities. Prevalent terms are devices, assets or tenants. Other terms are things, channels, agents, realms and nodes. In this context the capabilities to model entity relationships are investigated as well as the possibilities to separate and combine these components hierarchically. This led to following symbol-values for X_1:

$$X_1 = \{\text{none, basic, advanced, custom}\} . \tag{12}$$

The basic model allows no or only basic relationships and no methods to create a hierarchy. The advanced model offers a certain predefined set of relationships and allows hierarchy building. Finally, custom models allow free modelling that integrates a hierarchy.

Connectivity. The network connectivity summarizes mainly different technologies and protocols supported for edge communication. It is quantified by investigating the versatility of the supported protocols. On the one hand, there are *REST APIs* over *HTTP(S)* which are usually used for all other applications or general access. Nevertheless, it can also be used for edge communication, which is the typical realm for lightweight protocols. Examples would be *MQTT*, *CoAP* or *LoRa*. This led to following symbol-values for X_2:

$$X_2 = \{\text{specific, REST, lightweight, variety}\} \tag{13}$$

Specific represents the case, where only custom, non-standard protocols are provided. *REST* and *lightweight* are used, when only *REST* respectively only *REST* and one *lightweight* protocol is supported. *Variety* surpasses *lightweight* in the sense that multiple *lightweight* protocols must be supported. The weight ω_2 for this feature is set to $\frac{1}{2}$ because in our investigation, the usage of this feature for a strict capability differentiation was not that meaningful as all middleware systems provide a *REST API* and lightweight edge communication. The only difference is the variety of supported edge protocols.

Deployment. Deployment assumes that it is possible for the middleware and devices to discover each other e.g. over a broadcast and eventually establish a connection over respective communication protocols. The main difference between the remaining candidates is the degree of automation for handling of large quantities of devices. Deployment is quantified according to registration strategy for devices. This led to following symbol-values for X_3:

$$X_3 = \{\text{none, manual, self, bulk}\} \tag{14}$$

As in IoT, large scale scenarios can be assumed, handling of large quantities should get highest priority. Therefore, server-side bulk provisioning is the best rated strategy, followed by the strategy for devices to self-register. Due to lack of automation *manual* device registration is rated worst.

Persistent Communication and Message Handling. *IoT* middleware systems handle the communication of devices. Therefore, persistency, reliability and transmission time are important aspects. There are various approaches to communication handling, three popular solutions are used with the remaining candidates, that are *Apache Kafka*, *RabbitMQ* and *NATS (streaming)*. This led to following symbol-values for X_4:

$$X_4 = \{\text{none, custom, standard, variety}\} \tag{15}$$

None and *custom* are self-explanatory, whereas *standard* means that one of the three mentioned options and *variety* that a combination of those is used.

Security. In this step there are two security aspects considered: authentication and encryption. The main technologies are *OAuth* 2.0 for authentication and *TLS/SSL* for encryption. Other frequently used technologies are tokens e.g. *JWT* and certificates e.g. according to the X.509 standard.

This led to following symbol-values for X_5:

$$X_5 = \{\text{none, authentication, encryption, both}\} . \tag{16}$$

The values are self-explanatory, however the weight was chosen as $\omega_6 = \frac{1}{2}$ for this feature, because again, the usage of this feature for a strict capability differentiation was not that meaningful as the highest rated value was achieved by all candidates except of one.

User Management - Authorization. User management handles organization and access rights of users. In principle, a hierarchical organization by providing e.g. self-organization of subgroups is possible. Also, security and privacy issues can be addressed by customizing access rights and permissions of users, groups and roles.

This led to following symbol-values for X_6:

$$X_6 = \{\text{none, single, multiple, groups}\} \tag{17}$$

None represents an open system with no restrictions. *Single* stands for the case of full authorization on all resources after successful authentication. *Multiple* represents the case that between multiple users with different authorization capabilities is distinguished. Eventually, *groups* extends this capability by enabling to organize users in groups or attaching roles to them.

Data and Action Processing. Data and Action processing is commonly integrated in form of a rule engine. This rule engine allows defining data flow connections and conditions. A rule engine also allows filtering of data before transmission [9]. This feature is usually implemented and configured centrally.

This led to following symbol-values for X_7:

$$X_7 = \{\text{not supported, closed source, third-party, integrated}\} . \tag{18}$$

The selection of those values is based on the described elimination criteria to prefer open source solutions. Further, the preference of integrated solutions over third party components was chosen as compatibility issues are expected to be less likely.

Resilience Mechanisms. Device failures or loss of connection are scenarios that need to be considered as it is not possible to exclude them entirely. This feature is focused on reliability mechanisms, that step in if earlier measures for dependability fail [4]. Resilience mechanisms among other things consider failure or faulty data and that is addressed by providing alternative procedures or data sources. Options could be to increase physical devices [5] or communication links by using multicasting.

This led to following symbol-values for X_8:

$$X_8 = \{\text{no information, errors, device states, digital twin}\} . \tag{19}$$

The worst case is *no information* about the behaviour in a failure situation. A better reaction is for the system to report, e.g. via logging, *errors* so that a supervising instance can react appropriately. As an improvement, *device states* allow the system continue working with an alternative, possibly degraded, procedure. In general this requires human intervention. Presence of a *digital twin* option in a candidate receives the best rating. Digital twins simulate physical devices in the form of virtual replicas. This allows to make comparisons to predicted behaviour and detect faulty devices.

Scaling Technologies. Regarding scaling technologies, all suggested options in documentations were based on container technologies. Popular implementations are *Docker* with *Kubernetes* and *Helm Charts*, OpenShift or individual solutions like the *ThingsBoard* clustermode.

This led to following symbol-values for X_9:

$$X_9 = \{\text{set up, containerize, deploy, manage}\} . \tag{20}$$

Set up stands for no information about using container technologies. *Containerize* stands for official documentation on how to containerize special components. *Deploy* stands for available documentation on how to use the operational software (e.g. Kubernetes, Openshift) and *manage* for additional documentation about maintaining the operational software. The weight for this feature was adjusted to $\omega_9 = \frac{1}{4}$ as it can be classified experimental due to no official support being available to integrate the managing technologies.

Cloud Hosting Support. Arguments supporting cloud hosting capabilities encompass reducing expenditure of management or reducing unused hardware capacities. To check for those capabilities, support for public cloud hosting platforms like Amazon Web Services (AWS) or Microsoft Azure was checked. A typical use case for this feature is to transfer centralized core components and services that are not required at the edge to the cloud for more performant execution and management.

This led to following symbol-values for X_{10}:

$$X_{10} = \{\text{self, supported, managed, supported+managed}\} . \tag{21}$$

Self stands for non-availability of cloud hosting support. *Supported* stands for the possibility to integrate with a provider and have control over the offered resources, while *managed* describes the case where the control is outsourced to the provider. If both last named possibilities exist, then the value *supported+managed* is chosen.

Data Visualization. Visualizing data should comprise representing the gathered data in a suitable way to monitor past and current developments. Furthermore, it should provide the possibility to interact with the devices over a central interface. It is crucial that the middleware provides the possibility for customizing the interface according to individual requirements. This could range from

simple capabilities like data plotting up to highly customizing the entire graphical interface, also by integrating self-developed plug-ins, for larger projects.
This led to following symbol-values for X_{11}:

$$X_{11} = \{\text{not supported, closed source, third-party, integrated}\} . \qquad (22)$$

The selection of those values is based on the described elimination criteria to prefer open source solutions. Further, the preference of integrated solutions over third party components was chosen as compatibility issues are expected to be less likely.

Data Analytics. Data Analytics features allow getting further insights on the collected data by employing methods like grouping, aggregating, clustering, filtering or machine learning. A common approach for integration is to use open source Apache software like *Apache Spark, Apache Hadoop* or *Apache Storm*.
This led to following symbol-values for X_{12}:

$$X_{12} = \{\text{not supported, closed source, third-party, integrated}\} . \qquad (23)$$

The selection of those values is based on the described elimination criteria to prefer open source solutions. Further, the preference of integrated solutions over third party components was chosen as compatibility issues are expected to be less likely.

License Model. The following feature describes the license model of the middleware systems. The license is usually included in the source code repository and is valid for the entire content. Software usage comes with different legal obligations and restrictions for developers, which are commonly called the risk of infringement and risk of license restriction. Licenses that have low risks usually just require to keep the copyright notice in place. Classified as medium risk are licenses that additionally require to make the modifications open source. The highest risk have licenses that might require releasing other proprietary software under the same license as the open source license.
This led to following symbol-values for X_{13}:

$$X_{13} = \{\text{missing, high, medium, low}\} . \qquad (24)$$

The selection of those values follows the ordering of decreasing restrictions for modifications on the software.

Scalability and Stability Performance. The last investigated feature concerned Scalability and Stability Performance. To quantify this, we had to rely on previously conducted studies on solely 3 of the remaining candidates (*Thingsboard, Fiware* and *SiteWhere*). The first study [8] investigated message rates and error rates with different amounts of devices and parameters. The second study [6] is focused on the message rate, different amounts of publishing devices and differing amounts of message parameters.

This led to following symbol-values for X_{14}:

$$X_{14} = \{\text{no info, scalable (e), scalable (rc), scalable \& stable}\} , \qquad (25)$$

The selection of those values is based on the fact that it is a more desirable characteristic to scale the message rate without errors (e) and low resource-consumption (rc). Due to insufficient data (only two references considered), the weight was adjusted as follows: $\omega_{14} = \frac{1}{4}$.

5.3   Evaluation of Middleware Parts

In this section, we will present and evaluate the results of the Quantification Process. Table 2 shows the score for each feature for every individual middleware candidate. In addition, in the last row, the weighted overall score is presented. The evaluation of the 14 different features for *Mainflux, OpenRemote* and *Kapua* enables us to answer the second research question as, to the best of our knowledge, this was not done in related works.

Table 2. Quantitative evaluation of all features

	Mainflux	OpenRemote	SiteWhere	ThingsBoard	Kapua	Fiware	Node-RED
$f(x_1)$	1	2	2	2	2	3	1
$f(x_2)$	3	3	2	3	2	3	3
$f(x_3)$	3	1	2	3	3	2	1
$f(x_4)$	3	1	2	3	1	2	1
$f(x_5)$	3	3	1	3	3	3	3
$f(x_6)$	2	3	3	3	3	3	1
$f(x_7)$	0	3	3	3	0	2	3
$f(x_8)$	3	1	2	2	3	3	3
$f(x_9)$	3	2	3	3	2	3	2
$f(x_{10})$	2	2	1	3	2	0	3
$f(x_{11})$	2	3	1	3	2	2	3
$f(x_{12})$	2	0	1	1	2	2	2
$f(x_{13})$	3	1	2	3	2	1	3
$f(x_{14})$	0	0	1	3	0	2	0
$\sum_i \omega_i f(x_i)$	24.75	20.5	21.5	30.5	23.0	24.25	24.5

These results enable to evaluate following aspects:

Best Overall Rating. If the question on *What IoT middleware offers the best total package with respect to capabilities or feature-richness?* is posed, then our results can be utilized for an answer as a total ordering of middleware systems is provided. Our evaluation yields *Thingsboard* as the most promising candidate in this respect.

Selection Suggestion for Partial Aspect Prioritization. If a user is only interested in partial aspects respectively supported features, he could scan for individual feature ratings and prioritize them in his selection of a candidate. For example, if a small, securely operated IoT setup with performant data processing parts running in the cloud is required, then OpenRemote could be a fitting candidate. If a resilient solution, offering many Connectivity capabilities, is looked for, then Node-Red could be the choice.

Potentials for Feature Improvements. If a single developer or a team is eager to improve a special middleware, then our results give hints on which functionality, respectively feature, is missing or can be improved. For example, OpenRemote has a low resilience rating, which could be improved by providing an implementation of a digital twin service.

6 Conclusion

There are hundreds of IoT middleware systems, with a significant part being open sourced, available for operation today. If the application domain is not too narrow, it is a time consuming task to find a solution that fits the boundary conditions of the individual use case. We therefore presented a solution trying to tackle these challenges. To that purpose, we first proposed an efficient Selection Process which in the first step collected a vast number of IoT middleware systems before eventually iteratively reducing this number through simple binary conditions to a manageable number of remaining candidates. These candidates were then feature-wise quantified by a specially constructed mathematical model, which also provides the possibility to calculate a weighted sum of those features. The results of this quantification process can eventually be utilized to evaluate the *Best Overall Rating, Selection Suggestion for Partial Aspect Prioritization* and *Potentials for Feature Improvements*. Having successfully applied this approach manually in practice shows the feasibility of our methodology regarding complexity.

Opportunities for future work could comprise an in-depth comparison to other evaluation approaches, which might not necessarily target IoT middleware systems, but also software-frameworks from other operational domains. Furthermore, the different mappings and weights could undergo a better plausibility check by testing their individual functionality, though being complex, in practice and subsequently adjusting them. Further, the individual weights and mappings could be adjusted and more features added respectively removed if special IoT domains are considered. Finally, some parts of our approach could possibly be automated like the binary exclusion steps. Here, simple text-parsing techniques could come to the aid.

References

1. Borgia, E.: The internet of things vision: Key features, applications and open issues. Comput. Commun. **54**, 1–31 (2014). https://doi.org/10.1016/j.comcom.2014.09.008

2. Ccori, P.C., De Biase, L.C.C., Zuffo, M.K., da Silva, F.S.C.: Device discovery strategies for the IoT. In: 2016 IEEE International Symposium on Consumer Electronics (ISCE), pp. 97–98 (2016). https://doi.org/10.1109/ISCE.2016.7797388

3. da Cruz, M.A.A., Rodrigues, J.J.P.C., Al-Muhtadi, J., Korotaev, V.V., de Albuquerque, V.H.C.: A reference model for internet of things middleware. IEEE Internet Things J. **5**(2), 871–883 (2018). https://doi.org/10.1109/JIOT.2018.2796561

4. Delic, K.A.: On resilience of IoT systems: The internet of things (ubiquity symposium). Ubiquity 2016 (February), (February 2016). https://doi.org/10.1145/2822885

5. Eichhammer, P., et al.: Towards a robust, self-organizing IoT platform for secure and dependable service execution. In: Tagungsband des FB-SYS Herbsttreffens 2019. Gesellschaft für Informatik e.V., Bonn (2019). https://doi.org/10.18420/fbsys2019-03

6. Ghazala, A.A.E.D.I.: Systematic performance evaluation of internet of things middleware platforms. CU Theses (2019)

7. INFSO, D.: Networked enterprise and rfid infso g. 2 micro and nanosystems. internet of things in 2020, roadmap for the future (4) (2008)

8. Ismail, A.A., Hamza, H.S., Kotb, A.M.: Performance evaluation of open source IoT platforms. In: 2018 IEEE Global Conference on Internet of Things (GCIoT), pp. 1–5 (2018). https://doi.org/10.1109/GCIoT.2018.8620130

9. Kiran, M.P.R.S., Rajalakshmi, P., Bharadwaj, K., Acharyya, A.: Adaptive rule engine based IoT enabled remote health care data acquisition and smart transmission system. In: 2014 IEEE World Forum on Internet of Things (WF-IoT), pp. 253–258 (2014). https://doi.org/10.1109/WF-IoT.2014.6803168

10. Marques, G., Pitarma, R., Garcia, N.M., Pombo, N.: Internet of things architectures, technologies, applications, challenges, and future directions for enhanced living environments and healthcare systems: a review. Electronics (Switzerland) **8**(10), 1–27 (2019). https://doi.org/10.3390/electronics8101081

11. Molla, M., Ahamed, S.: A survey of middleware for sensor network and challenges. In: 2006 International Conference on Parallel Processing Workshops (ICPPW 2006), p. 6 p. 228 (2006). https://doi.org/10.1109/ICPPW.2006.18

12. Nastic, S., Truong, H.L., Dustdar, S.: A middleware infrastructure for utility-based provisioning of IoT cloud systems. In: 2016 IEEE/ACM Symposium on Edge Computing (SEC), pp. 28–40 (2016). https://doi.org/10.1109/SEC.2016.35

13. Ngu, A.H., Gutierrez, M., Metsis, V., Nepal, S., Sheng, Q.Z.: IoT middleware: a survey on issues and enabling technologies. IEEE Internet Things J. **4**(1), 1–20 (2017). https://doi.org/10.1109/JIOT.2016.2615180

14. Perera, C., Zaslavsky, A., Christen, P., Georgakopoulos, D.: Context aware computing for the internet of things: A survey. IEEE Commun. Surv. Tutorials **16**(1), 414–454 (2014). https://doi.org/10.1109/SURV.2013.042313.00197

15. Razzaque, M.A., Milojevic-Jevric, M., Palade, A., Clarke, S.: Middleware for internet of things: a survey. IEEE Internet Things J. **3**(1), 70–95 (2016). https://doi.org/10.1109/JIOT.2015.2498900

Pattern-Based Resolution of Integration Mismatches in Enterprise Applications

Jacopo Soldani$^{(\boxtimes)}$, Riccardo Paoletti, and Antonio Brogi

University of Pisa, Pisa, Italy
{jacopo.soldani,antonio.brogi}@unipi.it

Abstract. Modern applications integrate various heterogeneous software services, typically based on Enterprise Integration Patterns (EIPs). At the same time, such applications can include hundreds of interacting components, being these services or EIPs. This makes it complex to manually check whether the typed messages sent by a component to another are such that the latter can understand and suitably process them. We propose a design-time methodology for automatically identifying type mismatches in the messages exchanged among services and EIPs in a multi-service application. Our methodology also recommends how to refactor the architecture of a multi-service application to resolve the type mismatches therein. We assess the practical applicability of our methodology by presenting a proof-of-concept implementation, which we used to run a case study based on an existing, third-party application.

1 Introduction

Modern enterprise applications, e.g., microservices, integrate various heterogeneous services to deliver their functionalities [3]. This can be realised through the *pipes and filters* architectural pattern [11], due to which the overall application logic is partitioned among a set of nodes (called *filters*) connected through communication channels (called *pipes*). The nodes are not only the integrated services, but also the integration components used to let them interoperate.

Integration components typically implement EIPs, which allow a message-based integration of software services into an enterprise application [11]. For instance, there may be components implementing the *Recipient List* EIP to route the messages produced by a service to a set consumer services, or to select a subset of such consumers based on the messages' content, in accordance with the *Content-Based Router* EIP. Other examples are components filtering out some content from messages or translating it to match a different format, hence realising the *Content Filter* or *Message Translator* EIPs, respectively. EIPs may also be composed together, e.g., by exploiting a *Recipient List* to forward a message to multiple *Message Translators*, each transforming the message in a different format, which is that expected by the service that will consume it.

At the same time, modern enterprise applications may include hundreds of interacting nodes, being them services or EIPs, and this makes it complex to

Published by Springer Nature Switzerland AG 2022
F. Montesi et al. (Eds.): ESOCC 2022, LNCS 13226, pp. 93–108, 2022.
https://doi.org/10.1007/978-3-031-04718-3_6

check whether they are sending and receiving valid messages, viz., whether the messages sent by a service to another are typed so that the receiver can understand and process them. To determine whether this is the case, we must consider the composition of EIPs the messages go through. We must check each communication channel in the composition, by verifying that the message sent by the channel's source is compatible with the format expected by the channel's target. Due to the number and complexity of communication channels in modern enterprise applications, manually enacting such a mismatch resolution is costly, cumbersome, and time-consuming [23].

To this end, in this paper we propose a design-time methodology to identify and resolve type mismatches in multi-service applications. More precisely, we introduce a graph-based modelling for the architecture of an application, where typed nodes represent the application's *filters* (viz., its services and the EIPs used to integrate them), and where oriented arcs represent the application's *pipes* (viz., the channels among services and EIPs). Arcs actually connect a typed output of a node, representing the message it sends on the channel, to a typed input of another node, representing the message it expects on the same channel. Based on this, we define when a channel in an integration architecture denotes a type mismatch, and we provide an algorithm automatically identifying type mismatches. The algorithm also suggest refactorings enabling to resolve type mismatches in an integration architecture, with mismatch resolution based on replacing the channel denoting a mismatch with a composition of EIPs adapting the messages sent by the channel's source node to match the type of messages expected by the channel's target node, if possible.

We also present a proof-of-concept implementation enabling to identify and resolve type mismatches in integration architectures written in Apache Camel [2], the de-facto standard for enterprise application integration. We then showcase the practical applicability of our methodology by illustrating how we used its proof-of-concept implementation to run a concrete case study based on an existing, third-party integration architecture.

The rest of this paper is organised as follows. Section 2 provides a motivating scenario. Sections 3 and 4 introduce a modelling for integration architectures and an algorithm to automatically identify and resolve the type mismatches therein, respectively. Sections 5 and 6 present an implementation of our methodology and its use in a case study, respectively. Finally, Sects. 7 and 8 discuss related work and draw some concluding remarks, respectively.

2 Motivating Scenario

Consider the EIP-based loan broker proposed in [11], whose architecture is displayed in Fig. 1. The figure exploits the standard graphical notation for EIP-based integration [11], by modelling entry and exit points of the application as messages, and by exploiting coloured and white boxes to represent the involved EIPs and services' endpoints, respectively. The figure also displays the communication channels among such components, each drawn as an arrow to model the flow of messages from the arrow's source to its target.

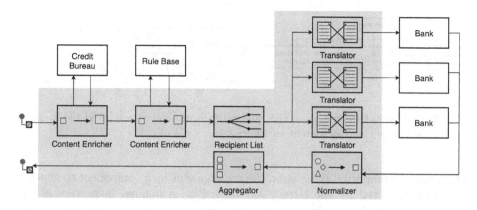

Fig. 1. An EIP-based loan broker [11].

The loan broker application starts with the loan request message received from a customer service. It then exploits a Content Enricher to forward information on the customer to the Credit Bureau service's endpoint, which returns the customer's credit score and history from the credit agency. This information, together with the information provided by the customer in her requests is passed to another Content Enricher, which interacts with the Rule Base service's endpoint to retrieve the most appropriate banks to contact for the loan. The Content Enricher then sends the original request together with the retrieved information to a Recipient List, which forwards the request to the selected subset of banks. More precisely, the Recipient List forwards the message to a set of Translators, which transform the message received to the format required by the selected Bank services. The Bank services's responses are then collected by a Normalizer, which transforms all responses to the format expected by the customer service, and then passes them to an Aggregator. The latter collects all normalized responses in a single message, which is finally returned to the customer service.

Consider now the very first channel in our EIP-based integration, which models the flow of incoming messages to the leftmost Content Enricher. Suppose that the received messages are structured as shown in Fig. 2a, whilst those that can be processed by the Content Enricher must be structured as shown in Fig. 2b.

When looking for the occupation of a customer, the Content Enricher will not find such information, despite the original message does include information on the job and income of the customer. This would hence result in an error being raised by the Content Enricher, which would stop the overall application's process. Currently, to discover such mismatch, we must manually compare the input messages with those expected by the Content Enricher, as per the specifications of both endpoints. We must then manually determine a suitable refactoring of our EIP-based integration that enables resolving the mismatch, e.g., by introducing additional EIPs to transform messages received on the entry point to match the format expected by the Content Enricher. We must actually repeat this process for identifying and resolving any possible mismatch in our application, by manually

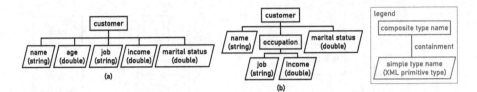

Fig. 2. Example of (a) message type received from the entry point and (b) message type expected by the first content enricher.

checking the compatibility between the message sent by a component to another and that expected by the latter, still relying on a manual inspection of the specifications of their endpoints. We must also ensure that all the integration components introduced to resolve identified mismatches are such that no new mismatch gets introduced as well.

The resulting mismatch resolution process is cumbersome, costly, and time-consuming [23]. To support developers in this direction, we hereafter present a design-time support that automatically discovers mismatches in EIP-based applications, by also recommending the adaptations enabling to refactor an application so that identified mismatches get resolved, if possible.

3   Modelling Integration Architectures

We hereafter introduce a formal modelling for integration architectures, which sets the foundations to analyse and resolve mismatches like that described in our motivating scenario. Mismatches occur when the type of a message sent on a channel is not compatible with that expected by the software component targeted by the channel. The messages flowing on a channel are indeed assigned with a given *named type*, which can be either simple or composite. Simple types are essentially assigning a name to an XML primitive type [18], whilst composite types essentially consist of a named container for multiple named types.

Definition 1 (Named Type). *Let $\mathcal{X}$ be the universe of XML primitive types. A named type is a pair $\langle n, x \rangle$, where*
– n denotes the type name and
– $x \in \mathcal{X} \vee x = \{t_1, \ldots, t_n\}$, with each t_i also being a named type.
We denote by $\mathcal{T}$ the universe of possible named types. We also denote by $\mathcal{T}^s = \{\langle n, x \rangle \in \mathcal{T} \mid n$ is a type name $\wedge x \in \mathcal{X}\}$ the universe of simple types and by $\mathcal{T}^c = \mathcal{T} - \mathcal{T}^s$ the universe of composite types.

Figure 3 provides an example of (a) simple and (b) composite types. The simple type models the names of multiple banks by exploiting the primitive XML type string. The composite type instead models the information on a customer of the loan broker application in our motivating scenario, with all such information being given through a set of simple types contained in the composite type

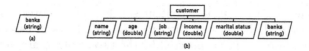

Fig. 3. Examples of (a) simple type and (b) composite type.

customer. Another example is given by the composite type customer in Fig. 2b, which not only contains simple types, but also another composite type.

Figure 2b and Fig. 3b also show how composite types essentially define trees, whose inner nodes are the names of composite types, and whose leaves are simple types. In the following, we assume composite types to be *finite*. We also abstract from the cardinality of inner types, assuming composite types constrain the inner types that must appear therein, but not how many times they should appear. For example, a message of type customer (Fig. 3b) must include at least an instance of the inner type job (viz., a string specifying a customer's job), but there can also be multiple instances of job if a customer has multiple jobs.

Simple and composite types enable defining the inputs and outputs that can be processed by the nodes in an integration architecture. An *integration node* is actually defined by its sort (viz., entry or exit point, EIP, or service endpoint), by the types of messages it expects on input channels, and by the types of the messages it sends to other nodes on output channels.

Definition 2 (Integration Node). *Let $\mathcal{M}$ be the set of message routing and transformation EIPs [11]. An* integration node *is a triple $\langle s, T_i, T_o \rangle$, where*
- *$s \in \mathcal{M} \cup \{\mathsf{endpoint}, \mathsf{entry}, \mathsf{exit}\}$ is the sort of the node,*
- *$T_i \subseteq \mathcal{T}$ is the set of input types, and*
- *$T_o \subseteq \mathcal{T}$ is the set of output types.*
We denote by $\mathcal{N}$ the universe of possible integration nodes.

An *integration architecture* is then modelled as a graph, whose nodes represent integration nodes. Each oriented arc instead models a channels, by connecting an output type t of a node to an input type u of another node. This is intended to model that the source node sends a message of type t to the target node on the corresponding channel, and that the target node is listening for messages of type u on such channel.

Definition 3 (Integration Architecture). *An* integration architecture *is a pair $\langle I, C \rangle$, where*
- *$I \subseteq \mathcal{N}$ is a finite set of integration nodes and*
- *C is a finite set of oriented channels,*
with $\langle i, \langle t, u \rangle, j \rangle \in C$ if $i = \langle \cdot, \cdot, T \rangle \in I$, $j = \langle \cdot, U, \cdot \rangle \in I$, $t \in T$, and $u \in U$.

Figure 4 provides an example of integration architecture, by displaying that of the application in our motivating scenario. For readability reasons, we omit to explicitly represent the structure of all input/output types in the integration architecture. Examples of such types are anyhow provided in Figs. 2 and 3, which provide the (a) output and (b) input types connected by the channels between the entry point and the leftmost content enricher, and between the rightmost content enricher and the recipient list, respectively. In both cases, we observe that the output/input types connected by the two channels are different, hence possibly causing type mismatches to be resolved.

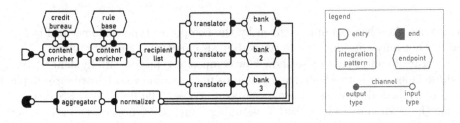

Fig. 4. Integration architecture of our motivating example.

To determine whether the difference between the output and input type connected by a channel denotes a mismatch, we must check whether the output type is *compatible* with the input type. Intuitively speaking, a type $\langle n, x \rangle$ is compatible with another type $\langle n, y \rangle$ if they have the same name and if x is in turn compatible with y. When x and y are both simple, they are compatible if they correspond to the same primitive XML type. Instead, when x and y are both composite, it must hold that, for each type in y, there must be a type in x that is compatible with such type.

Definition 4 (Type Compatibility). *Let $\langle n, x \rangle \in \mathcal{T}$ and $\langle n, y \rangle \in \mathcal{T}$ be two types. $\langle n, x \rangle$ is* compatible *with $\langle n, y \rangle$ (written $\langle n, x \rangle \geq \langle n, y \rangle$) iff*
- $x \in \mathcal{T}^s \wedge y \in \mathcal{T}^s \wedge x = y$ *or*
- $x = \{t_1, \ldots, t_n\} \wedge y = \{u_1, \ldots, u_m\} \wedge (\forall u_i \in y \,.\, \exists t_j \in x \,.\, t_j \geq u_i)$

The notion of *mismatch* directly follows from that of type compatibility: if a channel connects an output type t to an input type u, and if t is not compatible with u, then the channel denotes a mismatch.

Definition 5 (Mismatch). *Let $\langle I, C \rangle$ be an integration architecture. A channel $\langle i, \langle t, u \rangle, j \rangle \in C$ is a* mismatch *iff $t \not\geq u$.*

The notion of mismatch enables verifying whether an integration architecture is "valid", namely whether none of the channels therein denotes a mismatch. What if, instead, an architecture includes some mismatches? Can we resolve them?

4   Resolving Mismatches in Integration Architectures

We now introduce a methodology for automatically identifying mismatches in an integration architecture, and for resolving the mismatches occurring on channels starting from output types that can be adapted to match the target input types.

The idea is essentially the following: consider the mismatch denoted by a channel connecting an output type t to an input type u, with t that is not compatible with u. For the mismatch to be automatically resolved, it must be that t provides all the simple types that appear in u, but named or structured in a different way. If this is the case, we could resolve the mismatch by replacing the channel between t and u with a composition of EIPs that extracts the simple types from t, and which renames and reorganises such simple types to match type u.

Following the above idea, we first show how to determine whether a mismatch is "resolvable" (Sect. 4.1). We then show how to concretely adapt an integration architecture to resolve all resolvable mismatches (Sect. 4.2).

4.1 Resolvable Mismatches

To determine whether a mismatch is resolvable, we must determine whether the simple types in the available output type can be adapted to match those in the target input type. More precisely, for each simple type of the target input type, we must determine whether there exists a simple type in the available output type that represents the same concept with a compatible primitive XML type. We hence first introduce a function σ to denote the simple types contained in a type t. $\sigma(t)$ returns the singleton set $\{t\}$ when t is a simple type, whilst it returns the set of "leaves" of the tree defined by t when t is a composite type.

Definition 6 (Function σ). *Let $t \in \mathcal{T}$ be a type. The simple types in t are obtained with the function σ defined as follows:*

$$\sigma(t) = \begin{cases} \{t\} & if\, t \in \mathcal{T}^s \\ \bigcup_{u \in x} \sigma(u) & if\, t = \langle n, x \rangle \in \mathcal{T}^c \end{cases}$$

We can now formalize how to determine whether the mismatch denoted by a channel connecting an output type t to an input type u can be resolved. This essentially holds when each of the simple types in u can be mapped to at least one of the simple types in t, viz., when t is *adaptable* to u.

Notation. *We write $n \simeq m$ to denote that the type name n is semantically compatible with the type name m.[1] We also write $x \vdash y$ to denote that the primitive XML type x can be casted to y [18].*

Definition 7 (Adaptability). *Let $t, u \in \mathcal{T}$ be two types such that $t \not\simeq u$. t is adaptable to u (written $t \triangleright u$) iff*

$$\forall \langle n, x \rangle \in \sigma(u)\,.\,\exists \langle m, y \rangle \in \sigma(t)\,.\,n \simeq m \wedge x \vdash y$$

---

[1] A type name is semantically compatible with another if it represents the same concept or a sub-concept. We here rely on existing approaches to determine semantic compatibility between, like those surveyed in [5], for instance.

Algorithm 1: RESOLVEMISMATCHES($\langle I, C \rangle$)

1 $\langle I', C' \rangle \leftarrow \langle I, C \rangle$;
2 **for** $\langle i_o, \langle t_o, t_i \rangle, i_i \rangle \in C$ **do**
3   **if** $t_o \not\geq t_i \wedge t_o \triangleright t_i$ **then**
4          $\langle I', C' \rangle \leftarrow$ RESOLVEMISMATCH($\langle I', C' \rangle, \langle i_o, \langle t_o, t_i \rangle, i_i \rangle$);
5 **return** $\langle I', C' \rangle$;

Algorithm 2: RESOLVEMISMATCH($\langle I, C \rangle, \langle i_o, \langle t_o, t_i \rangle, i_i \rangle$)

1 $I' = \varnothing$;
2 $C' = \varnothing$;
3 **if** $t_i \in T^s$ **then**
4      $t = \pi(t_o, t_i)$;
5      $n = \langle \text{translator}, \{t\}, \{t_i\} \rangle$;
6      $I' = \{n\}$;
7      $C' = \{\langle n, \langle t_i, t_i \rangle, i_i \rangle\}$;
8   **if** $t_o \in T^s$ **then**
9          $C' = C' \cup \{\langle i_o, \langle t_o, t \rangle, n \rangle\}$;
10   **else**
11         $m = \langle \text{content filter}, \{t_o\}, \{t\} \rangle$;
12         $I' = I' \cup \{m\}$;
13         $C' = C' \cup \{\langle i_o, \langle t_o, t_o \rangle, m \rangle, \langle m, \langle t, t \rangle, n \rangle\}$;
14 **else**
15     $T = \{\pi(t_o, u) \mid u \in \sigma(t_i)\}$;
16     $m = \langle \text{content filter}, \{t_o\}, \{\langle \texttt{filtered}, T \rangle\} \rangle$;
17     $n = \langle \text{translator}, \{\langle \texttt{filtered}, T \rangle\}, \{\langle \texttt{translated}, \sigma(t_i) \rangle\} \rangle$;
18     $p = \langle \text{translator}, \{\langle \texttt{translated}, \sigma(t_i) \rangle\}, \{t_i\} \rangle$;
19     $I' = \{m, n, p\}$;
20     $C' = \{\langle i_o, \langle t_o, t_o \rangle, m \rangle, \langle m, \langle \langle \texttt{filtered}, T \rangle, \langle \texttt{filtered}, T \rangle \rangle, n \rangle,$
           $\langle n, \langle \langle \texttt{translated}, \sigma(t_i) \rangle, \langle \texttt{translated}, \sigma(t_i) \rangle \rangle, p \rangle, \langle p, \langle t_i, t_i \rangle, i_i \rangle\}$;
21 **return** $\langle I' \cup I, C' \cup (C - \{\langle i_o, \langle t_o, t_i \rangle, i_i \rangle\}) \rangle$;

4.2 Resolving Mismatches

Resolvable mismatches, viz., mismatches on channels starting from an output type that is adaptable to the targeted input type, can be resolved by exploiting the algoritm RESOLVEMISMATCHES (Algorithm 1). The algorithm essentially computes a refactoring $\langle I', C' \rangle$ of the integration architecture $\langle I, C \rangle$ by iterating over all its channels (line 2). If a channel $c = \langle i_o, \langle t_o, t_i \rangle, i_i \rangle$ denotes a mismatch (viz., $t_o \not\geq t_i$), whilst at the same time connecting an output type that is adaptable to the target input type (viz., $t_o \triangleright t_i$), RESOLVEMISMATCHES resolves the corresponding mismatch (lines 3–4). This is done by passing the architecture $\langle I', C' \rangle$ and the channel c whose mismatch must be resolved to the algorithm RESOLVEMISMATCH. The latter returns an updated architecture $\langle I', C' \rangle$ where the mismatch denoted by c is resolved (line 5).

RESOLVEMISMATCH (Algorithm 2) enables resolving the resolvable mismatch denoted by a channel c in an architecture $\langle I, C \rangle$. The algorithm essentially returns the original architecture, where the channel c denoting the mismatch has been removed, and where new nodes and channels (contained in sets I' and C', respectively) have been included to resolve the mismatch (line 21). Which nodes and channels to include actually depends on the target input type t_i, namely on whether t_i is simple (lines 3–13) or composite (lines 14–20).

When the target type is simple, viz., $t_i \in \mathcal{T}^s$ (line 3), RESOLVEMISMATCH introduces two new nodes, viz., a content filter m and a translator n, to obtain such simple input type from the available output type t_o. This is guided by the choice of the simple type in t_o selected to adapt t_o to match t_i, which in Algorithm 2 is modelled by a function π (line 4).[2] Intuitively, the content filter is used to extract from t_o the simple type selected to adapt t_o to match t_i, which is then renamed and/or casted by the translator to exactly match t_i. Whilst the translator is always introduced (lines 5–7), the content filter is introduced only if the output type is composite (line 10–13), as no filtering is needed if the available output type already consists of a simple type (lines 8–9). An example of application of RESOLVEMISMATCH is shown in Fig. 5a, where a channel connecting a composite output type to a single input type (in black) is replaced by a pipeline composed by a content filter followed by a translator (in grey). The figure also shows how the introduced content filter extracts the simple type value from the available output type price, and how the translator then renames value into cost to exactly match the input type expected by the receiver.

Instead, when the target type is composite (line 14), RESOLVEMISMATCH introduces a pipeline composed by a content filter m and two translators n and p, which adapt the available output type t_o to match the target input type t_i. This is again guided by the choice of the simple types in t_o selected to adapt t_o to match the simple types in t_i (line 15). The content filter m is introduced to obtain from t_o the set of filtered types selected to match the simple types in t_i (line 16). The translator n then generates a set of translated types, essentially by renaming and casting the filtered types to exactly match those in t_i (line 17). Finally, the translator p combines the simple types forming the *translated* types into a composite type structured in the very same way as the target type t_i (line 18). The nodes m, n, and p then constitutes the nodes I' to be added to $\langle I, C \rangle$, together with the channels C' used to structure the above described pipeline (lines 19–20). An example of use of RESOLVEMISMATCH to resolve the mismatch denoted by a channel connecting two composite types is shown in Fig. 5b. The figure shows how RESOLVEMISMATCH replaces a channel denoting a mismatch (in black) with a pipeline formed by a content filter and two translators. The figure also shows how the introduced content filter extracts the filtered types from manual, which are then suitably renamed by the leftmost translator

---

[2] π may be implemented by asking the developer to explicitly make the choices, or by picking the "most suited" simple type in t_o for each simple type in t_i based on some heuristics, e.g., based on the semantic similarity approaches surveyed in [5].

to obtain the `translated` types. The latter are then composed to obtain the target type `guide` by the rightmost `translator`.

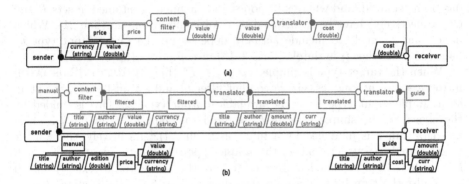

Fig. 5. Examples of mismatch resolution on channels targeting (a) simple and (b) composite input types. For readability reasons, refactorings are highlighted in grey, and the structure of composite types appearing multiple times is depicted only once.

The algorithm RESOLVEMISMATCHES is proved to be terminating, sound, and complete. Intuitively, soundness and completeness mean that whenever there is a mismatch on a channel connecting a node's output type to another node's input type, if such output type is adaptable to the input type, the mismatch gets resolved, whilst still preserving the connection between the two nodes and without introducing additional mismatches. In addition, the algorithm RESOLVE-MISMATCHES is proved to also be deterministic: independently from the order with which it considers the channels in the input architecture, it always computes the same refactored architecture.

5   Proof-of-Concept Implementation

We developed an open-source proof-of-concept implementation of our methodology, called MR[3] (*Mismatch Resolver*), which enables automatically identifying and resolving mismatches in the architecture of multi-service applications. MR essentially consists of an Angular-based GUI interacting with a Spring-based backend API. The latter implements all the logic for parsing EIP-based integrations programmed in Apache Camel [2], which are translated to the model presented in Sect. 3 and then analysed as described in Sect. 4. The GUI instead provides a graphical environment where to provide the necessary inputs, and it visualises the results of the analysis performed by the backend API.

Snapshots of MR's GUI are displayed in Fig. 6. It enables parsing an integration architecture, being this written in the Java DSL specified by Apache CAMEL [2]. The parsed architecture is then visualised, with integration nodes

---

[3] https://github.com/di-unipi-socc/MR.

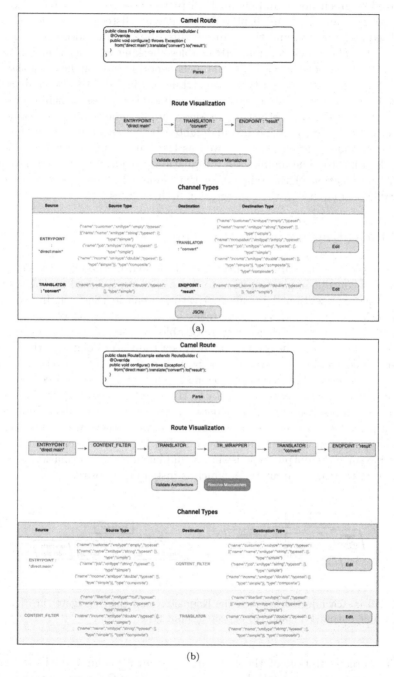

Fig. 6. Snapshots of MR's GUI, showing (a) a mismatch identified in an integration architecture and (b) the refactoring enabling to resolve such mismatch.

displayed as green boxes and channels displayed as arrows (Fig. 6a). The types being source and target of displayed channels are listed in a table below the visualised architecture, and they can be edited by opening ad-hoc dialogs.

With the above information, MR enables checking whether the architecture is valid. If this is not the case, the channels denoting mismatches and their corresponding source and target types are highlighted in red. MR also enables automatically determining how to resolve resolvable mismatches, which are resolved as described by RESOLVEMISMATCH (Algorithm 2). The refactoring enabling to resolve resolvable mismatches are highlighted by colouring in yellow the newly introduced nodes and channels, as well as the source and target types of such channels (Fig. 6b). The highlighted information provides application developers with a specification of the refactoring that should be implemented to resolve resolvable mismatches in their integration architectures.

6   Motivating Example Retaken

To assess the practical applicability of the proposed methodology, we exploited its proof-of-concept implementation to run a case study based on the loan broker application mentioned in our motivating scenario (Sect. 2). In particular, we artificially injected three mismatches in the specification of the loan broker application, two of which were resolvable, whilst one cannot be resolved. The resolvable mismatches were that between the Entry Point and the leftmost Content Enricher already described in Sect. 2, and one between the Normalizer and the Aggregator, for which we specified that the channel between them was connecting the output type in Fig. 7a to the input type in Fig. 7b. We instead injected a non-resolvable mismatch between the rightmost Content Enricher and the Recipient List, stating that the channel between them was connecting the output type in Fig. 3a to the input type in Fig. 3b. The latter mismatch is not resolvable since the output type is simple and lacking the information needed to reconstruct the target input type, which is instead composite.

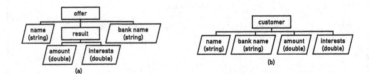

Fig. 7. Mismatch injected between the Normalizer and the Aggregator in Fig. 4, viz., (a) available output type and (b) expected input type.

The implementation of the loan broker application in Camel's Java DSL is publicly available on GitHub, together with the JSON representation of the types connected by its channels.[4] We loaded such implementation in the textbox

---

[4] https://github.com/di-unipi-socc/MR/UseCase.

at the top of MR's GUI, and we specified the channel types by means of the dialog opened by clicking on the *JSON* button. We then clicked on *Validate Architecture*, which effectively identified only the three mismatches we injected. We then clicked on *Resolve Mismatches*, obtaining that only the two resolvable mismatches were resolved, with the suggested refactoring (viz., the nodes and channels to include to replace the channels denoting the two mismatches) highlighted in yellow. The non-resolvable mismatch was instead left unmodified, but still highlighted in red to notify that it was still present.

7   Related Work

Type mismatch resolution has been widely studied in literature, with various existing techniques proposed to resolve mismatches in different contexts, e.g., [10] for programs, [4] for data-aware processes, or [16] for databases. Most of such techniques however differ from ours as they focus on nominal types, being these considered as singletons or in a list. Instead, in the context of EIP-based service integration, data assumes a tree-like format, amenable to a structural treatment, like those enacted in, e.g., [7,9], or [12]. Such a structural treatment inspired our solution to identify type mismatches in EIP-based multi-service applications, which we however aim at resolving by relying on EIPs themselves.

To this end, it is worth relating our solution to the existing solutions for rigorously engineering EIP-based multi-service applications. For instance, [1,8,13], and [24] propose four different solutions for obtaining multi-service applications by integrating different services through EIPs. [1] and [8] exploit model-driven engineering to compose EIPs to integrate the services forming an application, with [8] also enabling to automatically marshal the obtained integration architectures into executable Java programs. [13] introduces a planning-based method for integrating multiple services by generating executable compositions of EIPs. [24] proposes an unified modelling for the services and EIPs forming an application, by also allowing to transform modelled applications into executable application deployments. The above listed solutions however differ from ours since they focus on generating the compositions of EIPs allowing to integrate different services into a multi-service application. We instead enable analysing an EIP-based multi-service application to identify/resolve the mismatches therein.

In this perspective, [6,19], and [21] are closer to our proposal, as they all allow to analyse the EIP-based integration architecture of a multi-service application. They all share the baseline idea of mapping EIPs to an existing compositional modelling, viz., coloured Petri nets in [6], BPMN [17] in [19], and timed-DB nets [15] in [21]. [6] exploits coloured Petri nets to simulate an integration architecture, analyse its performances, and to verify whether it satisfies user-defined temporal properties. [19] instead shows how the mapping to BPMN allows to verify that messages effectively flows from a source to a target, passing through the EIPs used to integrate them. Finally, [21] analyses the timed-DB nets obtained from an integration architecture to check time-based properties and nets' safety and reachability. [6,19], and [21] hence complement the analysis we proposed, as they allow analysing different aspects of the design of an

EIP-based integration architecture, whilst abstracting from the actual types of messages exchanged among the services and EIPs forming the corresponding application. We instead focus on identifying and resolving the type mismatches in the messages exchanged among the services and EIPs in an application.

Differently from the above listed works, [20] explicitly takes into account the messages exchanged among the services and EIPs forming an application. [20] models EIP-based integration architectures with an extended version of control flow graphs, whose nodes model services or EIPs. Each node is also associated with its own outbound and inbound pattern contracts, describing the format of data it can send and receive, respectively. This information is then exploited to analyse runtime statistics and data flows. The analysis results are then used to estimate model complexity and to propose optimisations for an integration architecture, e.g., reducing the number of EIPs by replacing them with equivalente pattern compositions. [20] hence differs from our proposal in the objective, viz., optimising integration architectures, whilst we focus on identifying and resolving type mismatches in the messages among the EIPs and services therein.

In summary, there exist solutions for analysing multi-service application obtained by integrating multiple services through EIPs. These however either validate an integration by abstracting from the types of messages exchanged among services and EIPs [6,19,21], or consider such types but enact other analyses than mismatch resolution [20]. To the best of our knowledge, ours is hence the first solution enabling to identify and resolve type mismatches in the messages exchanged among the services and EIPs forming a multi-service application.

8 Conclusions

We presented a design-time methodology enabling to automatically identify and resolve type mismatches in multi-service applications. Our methodology is based on analysing a graph-based representation of the integration architecture of an application to automatically identify channels denoting type mismatches, and to resolve them by replacing their corresponding channels with compositions of EIPs, if possible. To assess the feasibility of our methodology, we also presented a proof-of-concept implementation of our methodology, which we then used to run a case study based on an existing application.

It is worth highlighting that our methodology currently enables identifying and resolving type mismatches in the *architecture* of a multi-service application. It indeed enables identifying the type mismatches in the communication channels of an application, by also suggesting the EIP compositions that can be used to resolve a mismatch by replacing the corresponding channel. The actual implementation of a mismatch resolution, that is, the concrete updates to be applied to the application sources, is left to application developer, much in the same way as the actual implementation of a design pattern is left to developers.

We anyhow plan to investigate how to exploit the semantics of EIPs to automatically generate the code implementing the refactorings resolving identified mismatches in an integration architecture. This could be done, e.g., by automatically generating the services implementing the logic for filtering/transforming the content of messages to match a target type. The Camel implementation of an integration architecture could then be automatically updated to include the newly generated services, hence finalizing the application refactoring.

Other directions we plan to pursue are performing a more thorough assessment of our methodology by applying to real-world, industrial case studies, and enhancing its usability (and that of its available implementation). As for the latter, we actually plan to enable automatically extracting the specification of the input/output types associated with each node. This can be done by relying on existing technologies for describing service interfaces, e.g., OpenAPI [14] or Swagger [22], which allow to determine the messages expected/returned by their endpoints, and by relying on the semantics of EIPs to determine how message flow and get transformed when passing through a composition of EIPs.

References

1. Al-Mosawi, A., Zhao, L., Macaulay, L.A.: A model driven architecture for enterprise application integration. In: Proceedings of the 39th Annual Hawaii International Conference on System Sciences (HICSS), vol. 8, pp. 181c–181c (2006). https://doi.org/10.1109/HICSS.2006.18
2. Apache: Camel. https://camel.apache.org. Accessed 25 Mar 2022
3. Bogo, M., Soldani, J., Neri, D., Brogi, A.: Component-aware orchestration of cloud-based enterprise applications, from TOSCA to docker and kubernetes. Softw. Pract. Experience 50(9), 1793–1821 (2020). https://doi.org/10.1002/spe.2848
4. Calvanese, D., Montali, M., Patrizi, F., Rivkin, A.: Modeling and in-database management of relational, data-aware processes. In: Giorgini, P., Weber, B. (eds.) CAiSE 2019. LNCS, vol. 11483, pp. 328–345. Springer, Cham (2019). https://doi.org/10.1007/978-3-030-21290-2_21
5. Chandrasekaran, D., Mago, V.: Evolution of semantic similarity-a survey. ACM Comput. Surv. 54(2) (2021). https://doi.org/10.1145/3440755
6. Fahland, D., Gierds, C.: Analyzing and completing middleware designs for enterprise integration using coloured petri nets. In: Salinesi, C., Norrie, M.C., Pastor, Ó. (eds.) CAiSE 2013. LNCS, vol. 7908, pp. 400–416. Springer, Heidelberg (2013). https://doi.org/10.1007/978-3-642-38709-8_26
7. Foster, J.N., Greenwald, M.B., Moore, J.T., Pierce, B.C., Schmitt, A.: Combinators for bidirectional tree transformations: a linguistic approach to the view-update problem. ACM Trans. Program. Lang. Syst. 29(3), 17-es (2007). https://doi.org/10.1145/1232420.1232424
8. Frantz, R.Z., Reina Quintero, A.M., Corchuelo, R.: A domain-specific language to design enterprise application integration solutions. Int. J. Coop. Inf. Syst. 20(02), 143–176 (2011). https://doi.org/10.1142/S0218843011002225
9. Gécseg, F., Steinby, M.: Tree languages. In: Rozenberg, G., Salomaa, A. (eds.) Handbook of Formal Languages, pp. 1–68. Springer, Heidelberg (1997). https://doi.org/10.1007/978-3-642-59126-6_1
10. Gil, J., Lenz, K.: Simple and safe SQL queries with c++ templates. Sci. Comput. Program. 75(7), 573–595 (2010). https://doi.org/10.1016/j.scico.2010.01.004
11. Hohpe, G., Woolf, B.: Enterprise Integration Patterns: Designing, Building, and Deploying Messaging Solutions. Addison-Wesley, USA (2003)

12. Hosoya, H., Pierce, B.C.: Xduce: a statically typed xml processing language. ACM Trans. Internet Technol. **3**(2), 117–148 (2003). https://doi.org/10.1145/767193. 767195
13. Mederly, P., Lekavý, M., Závodský, M., Návrat, P.: Construction of messaging-based enterprise integration solutions using AI planning. In: Szmuc, T., Szpyrka, M., Zendulka, J. (eds.) CEE-SET 2009. LNCS, vol. 7054, pp. 16–29. Springer, Heidelberg (2012). https://doi.org/10.1007/978-3-642-28038-2_2
14. Miller, D., Whitlock, J., Gardiner, M., Ralphson, M., Ratovsky, R., Sarid, U.: Openapi specification v3.1.0. https://spec.openapis.org/oas/v3.1.0. Accessed 25 Mar 2022
15. Montali, M., Rivkin, A.: DB-nets: on the marriage of colored petri nets and relational databases. In: Koutny, M., Kleijn, J., Penczek, W. (eds.) Transactions on Petri Nets and Other Models of Concurrency XII. LNCS, vol. 10470, pp. 91–118. Springer, Heidelberg (2017). https://doi.org/10.1007/978-3-662-55862-1_5
16. Quoc Viet Nguyen, H., Luong, X.H., Miklós, Z., Quan, T.T., Aberer, K.: Collaborative schema matching reconciliation. In: Meersman, R., et al. (eds.) OTM 2013. LNCS, vol. 8185, pp. 222–240. Springer, Heidelberg (2013). https://doi.org/10.1007/978-3-642-41030-7_14
17. OMG: Business process model and notation (BPMN) (2011). http://www.omg.org/spec/BPMN/2.0
18. Ray, E.T.: Learning XML, 2nd edn. O'Reilly, USA (2003)
19. Ritter, D.: Experiences with business process model and notation for modeling integration patterns. In: Cabot, J., Rubin, J. (eds.) ECMFA 2014. LNCS, vol. 8569, pp. 254–266. Springer, Cham (2014). https://doi.org/10.1007/978-3-319-09195-2_17
20. Ritter, D., May, N., Forsberg, F.N., Rinderle-Ma, S.: Optimization strategies for integration pattern compositions. In: Proceedings of the 12th ACM International Conference on Distributed and Event-Based Systems, pp. 88–99. ACM (2018). https://doi.org/10.1145/3210284.3210295
21. Ritter, D., Rinderle-Ma, S., Montali, M., Rivkin, A., Sinha, A.: Formalizing application integration patterns. In: 2018 IEEE 22nd International Enterprise Distributed Object Computing Conference (EDOC), pp. 11–20. IEEE (2018). https://doi.org/10.1109/EDOC.2018.00012
22. SmartBear: Swagger. https://swagger.io. Accessed 25 Mar 2022
23. Soldani, J., Tamburri, D.A., Van Den Heuvel, W.J.: The pains and gains of microservices: a systematic grey literature review. J. Syst. Softw. **146**, 215–232 (2018). https://doi.org/10.1016/j.jss.2018.09.082
24. Yussupov, V., Breitenbücher, U., Krieger, C., Leymann, F., Soldani, J., Wurster, M.: Pattern-based modelling, integration, and deployment of microservice architectures. In: 2020 IEEE 24th International Enterprise Distributed Object Computing Conference (EDOC), pp. 40–50 (2020). https://doi.org/10.1109/EDOC49727.2020.00015

Towards a Quality Model
for Cloud-native Applications

Robin Lichtenthäler$^{(\boxtimes)}$ and Guido Wirtz

Distributed Systems Group, University of Bamberg, Bamberg, Germany
{robin.lichtenthaeler,guido.wirtz}@uni-bamberg.de

Abstract. Cloud-native is a recent paradigm for web-based service-oriented applications. Because it covers a wide range of concepts and lacks a commonly accepted definition, evaluating software architectures according to it is difficult. Therefore, a quality model is presented, aligned with the Quamoco meta model and based on both practitioner books and scientific literature. It focuses on the design time and considers multiple quality attributes in relation. This initial quality model together with an evaluation of already existing measures is intended as a basis for approaches aiming to evaluate cloud-native application architectures.

Keywords: Quality Model · Cloud-native · Quality Attributes · Service-oriented

1 Introduction

Cloud-native as a software engineering paradigm for web-based service-oriented applications is popular nowadays as indicated by a recent survey [9]. Mentioned advantages of cloud-native include *improved scalability, shorter deployment time, improved availability* or *cost savings* [9]. To benefit from these advantages, developers need to understand what cloud-native means and be able to evaluate software architectures according to characteristics of the cloud-native paradigm. However, this is difficult, because cloud-native covers a broad range of aspects considering application design, development, deployment, and operation. Existing definitions of cloud-native applications [8,13,21,26,27,33] emphasize this breadth as they frequently contain enumerations of technologies, tools, design patterns, and development practices to apply. Even for the most notable definition of cloud-native applications by Kratzke and Quint [21], the authors state that it "*... can only be understood in a context of further terms...*" [21]. Our aim therefore is to conceptualize *cloud-nativeness* in the form of a quality model which structures the technologies, tools, design patterns, and development practices mentioned in the context of cloud-native applications by the quality aspects they impact (e.g., maintainability, reliability, or performance efficiency). This would enable developers to evaluate how design decisions impact quality aspects and highlight relationships between different quality aspects which has been

F. Montesi et al. (Eds.): ESOCC 2022, LNCS 13226, pp. 109–117, 2022.
https://doi.org/10.1007/978-3-031-04718-3_7

identified as important by Li et al. [23]. The goal of this work, constructing a quality model for cloud-native applications, is captured by the following two research questions:

RQ1: Which quality attributes can be assigned to cloud-native applications and structured in the form of a quality model?

RQ2: Which measures that have already been introduced can be used to measure the quality of a cloud-native software architecture?

With the first research question we want to derive the general quality attributes and their hierarchy. To apply the model, measures are needed, which are the aim of the second research question. We want to gain an overview of existing measures and map them to the derived quality attributes. This lays the foundation for future work in which we want to validate, refine and apply the model.

In the following, we describe related work in Sect. 2 and our methodology in Sect. 3. Resulting from that, our quality model is presented in Sect. 4 based on which we also evaluate the existence and need for measures. We discuss our findings and future work in Sect. 5, before ending with a conclusion in Sect. 6.

2   Related Work

An example of work focused on quality evaluations is the one of Ovaska et al. [25] who evaluate the quality in terms of reliability and security for single components based on their internal architecture. In contrast, our work aims at the level of several components interacting with each other. A more closely related topic therefore is that of the *microservices architectural style* [7]. In fact, from our point of view the topic of cloud-nativeness encloses the topic of microservices: The microservices architectural style focuses on the business domain of an application while cloud-nativeness also encloses additional cloud-focused, technical aspects. For evaluating the architecture of microservices-based systems, Cardarelli et al. [7] present an approach using a custom quality model focused on maintainability, however, without describing their measures in detail. A more detailed description of measures and their impacts on quality attributes is presented by Bogner et al. [6] who have used the Quamoco model to review and refine measures to evaluate the maintainability of microservices-based systems. Apel et al. [3] and Engel et al. [11] propose measures to rate the quality of microservices-based systems based on typically attributed characteristics, but with direct impacts from measures to high-level quality aspects, instead of an hierarchy of quality aspects. And Zdun et al. [37] define measures based on a formally defined representation of microservices-based systems to assess their quality based on the presence of typical microservices patterns. Finally, also focusing on cloud-native applications, Alonso et al. [2] describe the DECIDE H2020 project. However, their approach is based on recommending patterns for specified non-functional requirements [2] without a hierarchy of quality aspects or an explicit architectural model. The main difference of our work compared to the presented work is therefore that we propose an explicit quality model with a quality aspects hierarchy specific to the scope of cloud-native applications. Nevertheless, our work is interrelated especially with the work on microservices and we aim to also include their findings into our quality model for a solid foundation.

3   Methodology

In order to cover the thematic breadth of cloud-native, we started our quality model creation process (see Fig. 1) in a top-down manner with existing definitions for cloud-native applications [8,12,13,21,26,27,32,33,36] from both the academic literature and the industry. We extracted distinct statements about cloud-native characteristics (A) and mapped them to suitable quality aspects (B) of the ISO25010 standard [20] as a familiar and proven basis.

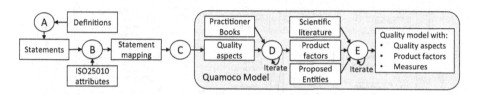

Fig. 1. Our approach for defining the quality model

As a foundation for our quality model we chose the Quamoco Quality Meta-Model [34,35]. Its core element is a *factor* being either a higher level *quality aspect* [35] (e.g., maintainability) or a *product factor* [35] which is an identifiable characteristic of a software system. Factors are ordered hierarchically so that multiple product factors can contribute to a quality aspect. We therefore transformed the statements into more specific quality aspects by combining similar statements and distinguishing separate concerns (C). As the topic of cloud-native is mainly driven by practice, we then scanned practitioner books [1,4,5,10,14,15,18,19,28–31] on the topic, because in contrast to other grey literature, they are at least to some extent reviewed before publishing. To derive product factors we mapped statements or chapters from the books to suitable quality aspects and iteratively refined our hierarchy of factors (D). Each factor characterizes an *entity* [35] of a software system which is in turn described as a set of interrelated entities. *Measures* [35] make product factors quantitatively measurable. In a bottom-up approach, we therefore proposed a set of entities suitable to capture the factors (E). And we performed a search of the scientific literature to find existing measures and evaluate their suitability to our model (E). Our criteria for selecting measures as suitable are that (1) a measure must consider the right level of abstraction, namely that of components and their interactions together with their technological basis (This explicitly excludes internal source code level measures) and (2) a measure must be calculable based on characteristics of the proposed entities. The literature search (described together with the whole methodology in more detail online[1]) lead to the identification of 61 papers

---

[1] https://github.com/r0light/cna-quality-model/tree/0.1.

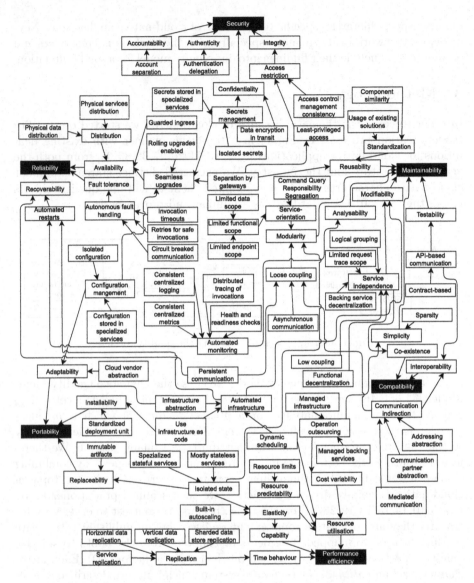

Fig. 2. A quality model for cloud-native application architectures

containing measures suitable to our model. We mapped these measures to the product factors and iteratively refined the model by also adding subfactors to product factors where measures revealed distinguishable factors within them.

4 A Quality Model for Cloud-Native Applications

The quality aspects and product factors of our proposed quality model for cloud native applications are shown in Fig. 2. The usage of the quality aspects from the ISO25010 standard [20] provides orientation and familiarity. We have put the top-most quality aspects at the edges with a black background for a better visualization of the different factor hierarchies. It has to be noted that we dropped the quality aspect of *functional correctness*, because it is not possible to evaluate it from an architectural point of view and we dropped *usability*, because our focus is on developers evaluating internal software architectures, instead of end users who have an external view on an application through its interface. Furthermore, we added a quality aspect named *simplicity* intended as the opposite to complexity, to accommodate products factors which are mentioned for reducing complexity.

Table 1. Number of measures proposed in the literature per product factor

Product Factor	No. of Measures and example
Limited data scope	2 (e.g., Service Interface Data Cohesion [6])
Limited endpoint scope	4 (e.g., Service Interface Usage Cohesion [6])
Mostly stateless services	4 (e.g., Ratio of stateless components [17])
Asynchronous communication	6 (e.g., Number of asynchronous outgoing links [3])
Persistent communication	2 (e.g., Service Link Persistence utilization metric [24])
Separation by gateways	3 (e.g., Externally available endpoints [38])
Distributed tracing of invocations	1 (Distributed Tracing Support [24])
Use infrastructure as code	1 (Lines of code for deployment configuration [22])
Low coupling	28 (e.g., Services Interdependence in the System [6])
Functional decentralization	10 (e.g., Service Criticality [6])
Limited request trace scope	3 (e.g., Service composition scope [38])
Backing Service decentralization	4 (e.g., Shared Storage Backing Service Interactions [24])
Sparsity	6 (e.g., Average Number of Endpoints per Service [6])
Service replication	2 (e.g., Service Replication level [16])
Horizontal data replication	1 (Storage Replication level [16])
Cloud vendor abstraction	1 (Service portability [16])
Isolated configuration	1 (Configuration externalization [3])
Immutable artifacts	1 (Number of Deployment Target Environments [3])
Physical Data distribution	1 (Number of Availability Zones used [16])
Physical Service distribution	1 (Number of Availability Zones used [16])
Retries for safe invocations	1 (Number of Links with retry logic [3])
Circuit breaked communication	1 (Number of Links with Complex Failover [3])
Mediated communication	3 (e.g., Service Interaction via Central Component [24])
Addressing abstraction	1 (Service Discovery Usage [3])

The impacts between factors are acyclic, as required by the Quamoco model [35], no factor occurs twice in the same hierarchy, and all factors that are not impacted by others are product factors. So far we only consider positive impacts, which is partly due to our analyzed literature where mostly desirable characteristics of cloud-native applications are discussed. As already mentioned, our quality model focuses on the design time of a cloud-native application, therefore we did not include product factors which can only be evaluated by analyzing the behavior of a system at runtime or factors considering aspects out of the core scope of an architectural point of view, such as the deployment process. This focus is expressed by two main aspects. One aspect is the choice of components and how they interact with each other. For example, *Limited functional scope* captures how services are designed in terms of how business functionality is distributed among services to ensure modularity. The other main aspect is how a system is designed to be deployed, that means on which kind of cloud infrastructure it is designed to run and how components are provisioned. For example, the factor *Automated infrastructure* captures how well the infrastructure on which components run is automated so that *automated restarts* are enabled to recover from a failure. We omit a detailed description of all factors and the entities which they characterize due to space constraints and refer the interested reader to our online representation of the quality model[2].

In addition to the factors and entities, measures are needed for an actual evaluation. In total, we found 88 suitable existing measures in the literature which we assigned to fitting product factors of our model. An overview is given in Table 1 which shows that we could assign measures to only 24 out of 53 product factors. Most measures that we found in the literature evaluate *maintainability* through the product factors *Low coupling* or *Functional decentralization*.

5   Discussion and Future Work

The quality model presented in Sect. 4 provides an overview on the desirable quality aspects and product factors of a web-based service-oriented application and how they can be achieved in a cloud-native architectural style, therefore answering **RQ1**. It provides a novel point of view, because multiple quality aspects are considered in combination. To use the model for a quantitative evaluation, however, measures are needed for which we provide an overview of suitable measures already presented in literature. As an answer to **RQ2** we can state that there is an imbalance in focus of existing measures, as there are numerous measures to evaluate maintainability in terms of coupling and cohesion, while for other aspects less measures exits. In future work, we therefore plan to propose and validate additional measures suitable to the product factors of our quality model. Furthermore, a threat to the validity of our model is that the relationships between factors of the model are based on our interpretation of the literature describing them. Additional work that validates the factors and

---

[2] https://r0light.github.io/cna-quality-model/.

their interrelations would improve the validity and may uncover additional relations. Empirical approaches, such as practitioner surveys or expert interviews are suitable approaches in this regard. Finally, the model should be used to evaluate software architectures in order to test its effectiveness and investigate the suitability of measures based on architectural models, because as also stated by Zimmermann: "...*it is an open research question how the usefulness [...] of architectural metrics in general could be evaluated.*" [38] An additional difficulty in this regard is the scope of our model. Because it currently comprises 103 factors, the outlined future work should also consider techniques to reduce complexity, for example by focusing evaluations on certain factor hierarchies or allow for setting parts of an architecture representation invisible when they are not in focus.

6 Conclusion

In this work, we present a quality model for architectures of cloud-native applications that is based on both practitioner books and scientific literature. It is a foundation for developing an approach to evaluate the quality of cloud-native application architectures. We found that there is an imbalance of quality attributes targeted by existing architectural measures for cloud-focused service-oriented software in the scientific literature and additional suitable measures are needed. But recent publications do address this topic and we think that it is a relevant field of research to which we want to bring more structure so that quality can be ensured in modern web-based service-oriented software.

References

1. Adkins, H., Beyer, B., Blankinship, P., Lewandowski, P., Oprea, A., Stubblefield, A.: Building Secure and Reliable Systems. O'Reilly, Sebastopol (2020)
2. Alonso, J., Stefanidis, K., et al.: Decide: an extended DevOps framework for multi-cloud applications. In: 3rd ICCBDC, pp. 43–48 (2019)
3. Apel, S., Hertrampf, F., Späthe, S.: Towards a metrics-based software quality rating for a microservice architecture. In: Lüke, K.-H., Eichler, G., Erfurth, C., Fahrnberger, G. (eds.) I4CS 2019. CCIS, vol. 1041, pp. 205–220. Springer, Cham (2019). https://doi.org/10.1007/978-3-030-22482-0_15
4. Arundel, J., Domingus, J.: Cloud Native DevOps with Kubernetes. O'Reilly, Sebastopol (2019)
5. Bastani, K., Long, J.: Cloud Native Java. O'Reilly, Sebastopol (2017)
6. Bogner, J., Wagner, S., Zimmermann, A.: Automatically measuring the maintainability of service-and microservice-based systems: a literature review. In: 27th IWSM, pp. 107–115. ACM (2017)
7. Cardarelli, M., Iovino, L., Francesco, P.D., Salle, A.D., Malavolta, I., Lago, P.: An extensible data-driven approach for evaluating the quality of microservice architectures. In: 34th ACM/SIGAPP Symposium on Applied Computing, ACM Press (2019)
8. CNCF: CNCF Cloud Native Definition v1.0. (2018). https://github.com/cncf/toc/blob/master/DEFINITION.md

9. CNCF: CNCF Survey 2020 (2020). https://www.cncf.io/wp-content/uploads/2020/12/CNCF_Survey_Report_2020.pdf
10. Davis, C.: Cloud Native Patterns. Manning, Shelter Island (2019)
11. Engel, T., Langermeier, M., Bauer, B., Hofmann, A.: Evaluation of microservice architectures: a metric and tool-based approach. In: Mendling, J., Mouratidis, H. (eds.) CAiSE 2018. LNBIP, vol. 317, pp. 74–89. Springer, Cham (2018). https://doi.org/10.1007/978-3-319-92901-9_8
12. Fehling, C., Leymann, F., Retter, R., Schupeck, W., Arbitter, P.: Cloud Computing Patterns. Springer, Vienna (2014). https://doi.org/10.1007/978-3-7091-1568-8
13. Gannon, D., Barga, R., Sundaresan, N.: Cloud-native applications. IEEE Cloud Comput. 4(5), 16–21 (2017)
14. Garrison, J., Nova, K.: Cloud Native Infrastructure. O'Reilly, Sebastopol (2017)
15. Goniwada, S.R.: Cloud Native Architecture and Design Patterns. In: Cloud Native Architecture and Design, pp. 127–187. Apress, Berkeley (2022). https://doi.org/10.1007/978-1-4842-7226-8_4
16. Guerron, X., Abrahao, S., Insfran, E., Fernandez-Diego, M., Gonzalez-Ladron-De-Guevara, F.: A taxonomy of quality metrics for cloud services. IEEE Access 8, 131461–131498 (2020)
17. Hirzalla, M., Cleland-Huang, J., Arsanjani, A.: A metrics suite for evaluating flexibility and complexity in service oriented architectures. In: Feuerlicht, G., Lamersdorf, W. (eds.) ICSOC 2008. LNCS, vol. 5472, pp. 41–52. Springer, Heidelberg (2009). https://doi.org/10.1007/978-3-642-01247-1_5
18. Ibryam, B., Huß, R.: Kubernetes Patterns. O'Reilly, Sebastopol (2020)
19. Indrasiri, K., Suhothayan, S.: Design Patterns for Cloud Native Applications. O'Reilly, Sebastopol (2021)
20. ISO/IEC: ISO/IEC 25000 Systems and software engineering - Systems and software Quality Requirements and Evaluation (SQuaRE) (2014). https://www.iso.org/standard/64764.html
21. Kratzke, N., Quint, P.C.: Understanding cloud-native applications after 10 years of cloud computing - a systematic mapping study. JSS 126, 1–16 (2017)
22. Lehmann, M., Sandnes, F.E.: A framework for evaluating continuous microservice delivery strategies. In: 2nd ICC, ACM (2017)
23. Li, S., et al.: Understanding and addressing quality attributes of microservices architecture: a systematic literature review. Inf. Softw. Technol. 131, 106449 (2021)
24. Ntentos, E., Zdun, U., Plakidas, K., Meixner, S., Geiger, S.: Metrics for assessing architecture conformance to microservice architecture patterns and practices. In: Kafeza, E., Benatallah, B., Martinelli, F., Hacid, H., Bouguettaya, A., Motahari, H. (eds.) ICSOC 2020. LNCS, vol. 12571, pp. 580–596. Springer, Cham (2020). https://doi.org/10.1007/978-3-030-65310-1_42
25. Ovaska, E., Evesti, A., Henttonen, K., Palviainen, M., Aho, P.: Knowledge based quality-driven architecture design and evaluation. IST 52(6), 577–601 (2010)
26. Pahl, C., Jamshidi, P., Zimmermann, O.: Architectural principles for cloud software. ACM Trans. Internet Technol. 18(2), 1–23 (2018)
27. RedHat: Understanding cloud-native applications (2018). https://www.redhat.com/en/topics/cloud-native-apps
28. Reznik, P., Dobson, J., Gienow, M.: Cloud Native Transformation. O'Reilly, Sebastopol (2019)
29. Richardson, C.: Microservices Patterns. 1 edn. Manning, Shelter Island (2019)
30. Ruecker, B.: Practical Process Automation. O'Reilly, Sebastopol (2021)
31. Scholl, B., Swanson, T., Jausovec, P.: Cloud Native. O'Reilly, Sebastopol (2019)

32. Toffetti, G., Brunner, S., Blöchlinger, M., Spillner, J., Bohnert, T.M.: Self-managing cloud-native applications: design, implementation, and experience. Future Gener. Comput. Syst. **72**, 165–179 (2017)
33. VMwareTanzu(Pivotal): Cloud-Native Applications: Ship Faster, Reduce Risk, Grow Your Business (2020). https://tanzu.vmware.com/de/cloud-native
34. Wagner, S., et al.: Operationalised product quality models and assessment: the Quamoco approach. IST **62**, 101–123 (2015)
35. Wagner, S., et al.: The quamoco quality meta-model. techreport TUM-I128, Technische Universität München, Institut für Informatik (2012)
36. Wurster, M., Breitenbücher, U., Brogi, A., Leymann, F., Soldani, J.: Cloud-native Deploy-ability: an analysis of required features of deployment technologies to deploy arbitrary cloud-native applications. In: 10th CLOSER. Scitepress (2020)
37. Zdun, U., Navarro, E., Leymann, F.: Ensuring and assessing architecture conformance to microservice decomposition patterns. In: Maximilien, M., Vallecillo, A., Wang, J., Oriol, M. (eds.) ICSOC 2017. LNCS, vol. 10601, pp. 411–429. Springer, Cham (2017). https://doi.org/10.1007/978-3-319-69035-3_29
38. Zimmermann, O.: Metrics for architectural synthesis and evaluation - requirements and compilation by viewpoint. an industrial experience report. In: IEEE/ACM 2nd International Workshop on Software Architecture and Metrics, IEEE (2015)

Serverless

Upilio: Leveraging the Serverless Paradigm for Building a Versatile IoT Application

Markus Mock[✉] and Stefan Arlt

University of Applied Sciences Landshut, Landshut, Germany
{Markus.Mock,Stefan-Alexander.Arlt}@haw-landshut.de

Abstract. Serverless computing has emerged over the last couple of years as a flexible paradigm for deploying cloud-based applications and allowing developers to focus on their applications and reduce application maintenance costs over the lifetime of an application. However, there has not been an examination of whether a complex application can be built and operated with high performance and low operating cost relying entirely on the serverless paradigm. This paper presents the design, implementation, performance, and cost evaluation of what we believe to be a representative kind of IoT application, a cloud-based energy data management system named Upilio. Upilio is a versatile data collection and analysis platform for IoT sensor data. Upilio's functionality is implemented entirely using AWS Lambda serverless functions and managed services to store data, and even the graphical user interface does not need a dedicated web server. Our empirical evaluation shows that the system, including its serverless online analytics (OLAP) functionality, is cost-effective, requiring only a fraction of the server cost necessary for operating such a system using on-premise hardware. Thus, Upilio demonstrates that complex IoT system scenarios can be implemented successfully with good performance and cost characteristics leveraging the serverless paradigm.

Keywords: Serverless Computing · FaaS · IoT

1 Introduction

Over the past fifteen years, cloud computing has fundamentally changed the computing landscape. Many applications that were traditionally run on-premises have moved to the cloud and are now often delivered as Software-as-a-Service (SaaS). Due to the unprecedented scale and elasticity of cloud computing resources and the ensuing agility, many new and entirely cloud-based companies have been created. While cloud computing has liberated those companies from procuring, upgrading, and maintaining their hardware, they typically still need to configure their servers and operating systems hosted by their cloud provider of choice to be able to run their applications.

© IFIP International Federation for Information Processing 2022
Published by Springer Nature Switzerland AG 2022
F. Montesi et al. (Eds.): ESOCC 2022, LNCS 13226, pp. 121–136, 2022.
https://doi.org/10.1007/978-3-031-04718-3_8

Recently, serverless computing [16] has emerged as a new paradigm for deploying cloud-based applications with the promise of unburdening application developers even from configuring and scaling their cloud-based servers and instead enabling them to concentrate entirely on their application. Additionally, as computing time is only incurred when a function is performed, serverless computing also comes closer to deliver the original promise of cloud computing of paying only for actually used resources coupled with virtually infinite scalability. Moreover, due to the event-driven programming model, serverless computing also seems ideally matched to the implementation of IoT applications, which need to perform computations whenever new sensor data is produced.

However, while this technology has enormous potential, there are also challenges. For instance, there has been concern about potentially high operational costs due to the new billing model (e.g., [18]) and problems created due to storage disaggregation [30]. This paper examines whether a practical IoT application can be implemented with both good performance and cost-efficacy. We investigate the efficacy of using AWS Lambda for building a practical application that solves a vital real-world problem, namely energy (data) management. More importantly for our purposes, in addition to its practical relevance, we also believe that a cloud-based energy data processing system that collects, stores, and enables manual and automatic analytical operations on energy-consumption and production data is a good benchmark for evaluating the serverless paradigm for its viability for building complex practical applications because it combines continuous data collection from an IoT sensor system with analytical functionality and a graphical user interface to interact with the system.

To investigate how well the serverless paradigm can address these varied demands, we designed and implemented Upilio.[1] Upilio implements the data collection and monitoring part of an energy management system (EMS) for buildings by combining various simple data ingest, storage, and processing functions as AWS Lambda code to collect and store EMS data in real-time. It continuously applies machine-learning algorithms to produce and update predictions of energy consumption and production.

We evaluate the performance and cost-effectiveness of Upilio based on a workload that is typical for our university environment. We extract the relevant cost components and extrapolate operating costs to both higher and lower demands and show that Upilio operates cheaply even for large sites with many buildings and sensors with high data velocity. Combined with its extensibility and easy deployment, we conclude that Upilio and similar IoT applications can be implemented using the serverless paradigm with excellent cost and scaling characteristics.

This paper makes the following contributions:

– It provides a demonstration of how a complex real-world application can be implemented entirely using serverless technology.

---

[1] Upilio is Latin for "shepherd"; the Upilio system takes care of the users' sensor data in the cloud.

- It shows that with serverless technology combined with the infrastructure-as-code approach, a sophisticated system can be deployed and operated without first building a costly on-premise infrastructure and how updates to the edge sensor configuration can be performed from the cloud.
- It shows how a versatile web-based graphical user interface that is available 24/7 can be realized without dedicated web server hardware, i.e., serverlessly.
- It presents a blueprint for building scalable and versatile serverless IoT applications.
- Finally, the paper demonstrates that the system, including serverless OLAP functionality is cost-effective, requiring only a fraction of the server cost for operating the system on-premise hardware.

The remainder of the paper is structured as follows: after reviewing background and related work, Sect. 3 provides an overview of the Upilio system and its operating environment and provides details on how the analytics operations for OLAP and the graphical user frontend are implemented serverlessly. Section 4 provides an experimental evaluation demonstrating the benefits and cost-effectiveness of our approach and Sect. 5 provides conclusions.

2   Background and Related Work

Serverless computing has been receiving much attention recently as a potential fulfillment of cloud computing's original promise of liberating users from the burden of procuring and managing hardware and software (operating) systems and letting them instead focus entirely on their application-level code. Besides some open-source approaches, which still require someone to host and run the platform, many commercial offerings have emerged over the past years; for a comparison consult for instance [24]. Castro et al. [16] offer the following definition: "Serverless computing is a platform that hides server usage from developers and runs code on-demand automatically scaled and billed only for the time the code is running." They distinguish this general definition from a specific embodiment, namely Function-as-a-Service (FaaS), which however is often used interchangeably in the literature but, which narrowly defined, is a subset of serverless computing where the unit of computation are functions, which are executed typically in response to some event. AWS Lambda [11] is a commercial offering of a FaaS platform on top of which we have built Upilio. Using AWS Lambda, developers write code without considering on what hardware it will be executed.

Applications are broken into separate functions, which can be implemented in a variety of programming languages, e.g., Javascript, Java, Go, or Python; for Upilio, we have used the Python language. Users are billed in 100 ms-increments for actual compute resource usage and a Lambda function can execute for at most 900 s. The maximum memory available to the function has to be specified when a Lambda function is deployed; the selected memory determines the billing rate. The more memory is configured, the higher the CPU performance that the function is executed on; an independent selection of the two is impossible.

These Lambda functions are executed in lightweight containers [1] providing portability and security, as well as virtually unlimited scalability since the functions can be executed on as many machines as are available, and the user is willing to pay for. Other commercial cloud providers besides Amazon offer similar FaaS offerings, e.g., Google Cloud Functions [19] or Microsoft Azure Functions [14]. A primary advantage of the FaaS model is its simple event-driven programming model.

One recent development in IoT data processing is applying the FaaS model to the IoT domain to take advantage of the convenient programming model and the excellent scalability properties. Open-source offerings such as Apache Whisk [4] and commercial platforms such as AWS Greengrass [10] provide an execution environment for specific edge devices, thereby making it possible to execute functions that were initially written for the FaaS cloud platform at the edge. AWS Greengrass is a framework with a collection of software libraries that enables the execution of Lambda functions on IoT devices that are Greengrass-enabled. In Upilio, we run the Greengrass core system on Raspberry PI single-board computers that serve as data collectors at the edge (cf. Sect. 3.1). Greengrass provides the software engineering benefit of code reuse, as many Lambda functions written for the cloud can be executed unchanged on the edge devices. Lambda functions running on IoT devices can process data, execute cloud messaging operations and even perform learning inference operations and AWS Greengrass provides some prebuilt components to facilitate the development of such edge functionalities.

One additional advantage of the AWS Greengrass platform is that Lambda functions and configuration files can be deployed and updated from the Greengrass cloud service. This capability frees developers of edge applications from writing their own software management and update platform and from the time-consuming process of manually updating the software and configuration settings at multiple edge devices whenever a change is required, thereby increasing the agility of edge applications and reducing operational costs.

Aslanpour et al. [5] have looked more generally at the opportunities and challenges of applying the serverless paradigm to edge computing and, therefore, to IoT scenarios. Like others, they also point out the excellent match between the event-driven nature of IoT applications and the serverless programming model. However, on the downside, they also point out that high latency due to cold-start issues can be problematic for some applications.

Baresi et al. [15] propose a serverless architecture for a specific edge computing use case, namely mobile augmented reality. Using IBM's OpenWhisk serverless framework [23] in locally located servers, they compare the latency and general performance of their augmented reality application when executing the functions that provide a reality augmentation serverlessly in the cloud or at the edge. As expected, the latencies at the edge are lower than in cloud-based FaaS systems. However, their approach required them to set up their own edge serverless environment. In our approach, we are leveraging AWS Lambda's Greengrass integration, which allows the execution of serverless functionality at the edge, on Greengrass-enabled devices, Raspberry PI single-board computers in our setup.

Wang et al. [31] present LaSS, an architecture for running latency-sensitive serverless applications at the edge. They use a queuing-theoretic framework to allocate resources to containers executing serverless functions to ensure that latency goals are met. They used OpenWhisk to implement a prototype of their system and evaluated it using a benchmark consisting of a handful of different latency-critical applications. Their work should be valuable to cloud providers for extending existing public clouds to support latency-critical serverless functions, precisely when those can be executed at the edge, such as AWS Greengrass or Azure IoT. There were no aggressive latency demands in our examine use case requiring edge execution. However, some IoT application scenarios do require ensuring maximum latencies. Currently, in AWS Greengrass edge execution, this can only be achieved by proper provisioning at the edge and potential overprovisioning as you would when operating a serverful application.

One step towards solving this overprovisioning problem for a public cloud is Pelle et al.'s work [26]. They propose a middleware layer for AWS Greengrass, which receives application-specific performance metrics and uses this information to change the edge configuration, e.g., by changing the placement of Lambda function execution on edge devices. They evaluate their system using simulations. However, how well the (positive) simulation results translate to an implemented system needs to be evaluated.

An actual prototypical serverless platform specifically for edge computation is presented and evaluated by Pfandzelter and Bermbach [27]. Their design is specifically geared towards resource efficiency and meant to run on single-board computers. They present a prototype implementation using Docker containers to place function handlers and a management service running on each edge host directly. To reduce resource requirements and latency, clients perform requests using the CoAP protocol, which is used in many IoT systems, rather than HTTP resulting in lower latency as CoAP is based on UDP transport rather than TCP. Their experimental comparison found that their platform introduced only minimal overhead compared to native Node.js execution.

Upilio, like many IoT scenarios, also requires performing analytics operations on the acquired sensor data. There has been a fair amount of work looking at serverless analytics. For instance, Nastic et al. [25] present a combined cloud and edge real-time data analytics platform that can perform analytics both at the edge and in the cloud. Simpler and latency-critical functions are executed at the edge, while more complex analytics can be executed in the cloud. Their model proposes processing the edge real-time data serverlessly. To facilitate that, they propose an extension of what they label the traditional streams model by adding serverless data analytic functions into the data stream. In contrast to some of their application domains, e.g., vital signs monitoring in a medical context, the latency imposed by transmission to the cloud is generally immaterial for a cloud-based energy management system such as Upilio. However, their proposal is similar to Upilio's approach since we also execute simple processing functions at the edge using the AWS Greengrass core as described in Sect. 3.1. Simple anomaly detection methods can be executed at the edge so that energy consumption anomalies can also be detected directly at the edge without data transmission to the cloud.

3   Upilio: Design and Implementation

In order to make our results as generalizable as possible, Upilio's architecture follows these design goals. First, the system had to be able to accommodate heterogeneous sensor equipment, as is typically found when buildings are instrumented with energy sensors and are not built with instrumentation from scratch. However, even in the latter case, being able to switch suppliers to avoid provider lock-in is desirable. Moreover, since our architecture is built for heterogeneity, it also applies to other IoT sensor scenarios. Second, the system has to be easy to deploy without expensive capital investments and minimal operational demands. While automated control was not a requirement for our pilot system, the design still has to be extensible to allow for automated control, which motivated our choice of leveraging the AWS IoT Greengrass platform for our data collection operations as it enables us to execute some analyses, e.g., anomaly detection, at the edge as well; a requirement that many general IoT applications share as well. In addition, it is desirable that the fleet of IoT devices can be (re-) configured and updated from the cloud to minimize personnel costs.

Upilio is used to collect, store and process energy- and resource-related data from our university's three campuses, the main campus located in Landshut and two satellite campuses located in Lower Bavaria. To limit the number of data connections from each site and provide an opportunity for trading off data freshness and communication bandwidth, again a requirement shared by many IoT scenarios, measurement devices do not communicate directly with the Upilio cloud backend. Instead, each site uses one (and, for large sites, potentially multiple instances to avoid bottlenecks) data collector for which we use Raspberry Pi [28] single-board computers. They also serve as Greengrass core devices as explained in Sect. 3.1. Currently, at the main campus, Upilio is continuously ingesting data from approximately one hundred sensors. They measure electricity consumption in various buildings and laboratories, measuring both power consumption and aggregate energy use, taking measurements every minute. Regional heat and water consumption, again at building and sub-building levels, are measured in 15-min intervals. Besides, the university has solar panels and the electricity production from this installation with a peak power of 100 kW is measured every minute, as is weather data from an on-campus weather station, which measures global irradiance, temperature, and relative humidity at several ground levels.

The remainder of this section describes how we leveraged the serverless paradigm in Upilio's design and implementation in more detail and presents the reference architecture that should be usable as a blueprint for similar IoT sensor scenarios. Section 3.1 describes how data is represented and collected at the edge. Section 3.2 describes the data ingress APIs and Sect. 3.3 how the web-based

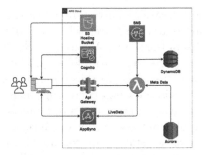

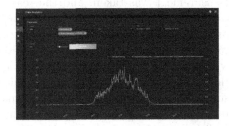

Fig. 1. Upilio frontend architecture. The serverless web frontend is implemented with static Javascript code in S3 buckets calling Lambda functions on REST APIs.

Fig. 2. A view of Upilio's analytics dashboard showing a combination of the photovoltaic energy produced at the main campus on the selected 24 h period overlayed with the global radiation, both normalized to display them at the same scale.

GUI was implemented serverlessly. Finally, Sect. 3.4 describes how analytics was implemented.

3.1 Data Representation and Real-Time Collection

To enable the use of sensors from different manufacturers that represent data in different formats and to be able to incrementally add new sensors to a running system without interrupting its operations, an essential requirement for our Upilio design was for it to be extensible. Adding a new sensor type should not require any code changes to the existing storage and processing backend. Moreover, it is essential to be able to change the frequency of measurements without manually updating configuration files at each sensor site because typically, sensors are located in utility tunnels or access-restricted locations so that updating them in situ is cumbersome. Furthermore, there are bound to be many sensors, and updating them all one by one would be laborious.

Data Representation. Interface definition languages (IDLs) are a well-known mechanism for representing data types in an extensible and portable way. We chose to use the Thrift IDL language [2], which is a language-neutral, platform-neutral, and extensible mechanism for serializing structured data in a compact and efficient form. Thrift comes with tools to automatically create serialization and deserialization code stubs from the data type description. Data types can be updated by adding additional (optional) struct fields without breaking the existing processing code.

Every sensor device is assigned a unique device id and its measurement value is represented as a double value. Also, two (Unix) timestamps are recorded:

the sensor timestamp, a timestamp set by the sensor, which records when the measurement was taken, and the reading timestamp, which records when the collector node (=RPI) reads the sensor value from the sensor. We use the NTP protocol to keep the clocks of our collector nodes synchronized to UTC so that we can correlate measurements taken at different sensors based on their timestamp within the NTP-synchronization accuracy, which is in the millisecond range more than sufficient for the frequency at which energy consumption needs to be measured. From this primary data type, more complex data types, for instance, to represent the collection of measurements of a weather station are composed. In addition, all of our data type definitions carry a version number making rolling updates to new definitions possible. This data representation should cover most sensor IoT scenarios, not just our concrete use case.

Edge Data Collection in Upilio. Upilio uses the AWS Greengrass platform to enable the execution of Lambda functions both in the cloud and at the edge. At every campus location, at least one Raspberry PI device serves as a data collector. Using the Greengrass platform provides two advantages: first, we can avoid reimplementing functionality that can be useful both in the cloud and the edge. For example, we can perform some simple anomaly detection both in the cloud and at the edge, using Arima (cf. [22] for details on anomaly detection in Upilio). The ability to perform monitoring or analysis operations at the edge is crucial for detecting unusual operating conditions even when Internet connectivity is lost or would have too high a latency. While Upilio does not drive any automatic control systems, this capability would be indispensable in such a case. Another crucial advantage afforded by Greengrass is that it enables us to update both the function implementation and the configuration files from the cloud. Furthermore, we can deploy updated code or configuration files reliably without implementing our own update mechanism, which, for instance, enables us to update the collection frequency in selected buildings without the need to access the RPI computers, which are mostly co-located with sensors in utility rooms and tunnels that are difficult to access and access-controlled.

Note that these two requirements of being able to perform latency-sensitive operations and being able to operate when Internet connectivity is lost is shared in many other IoT scenarios. Furthermore, configuration and code updates from the cloud are an important requirement in many scenarios as well, therefore being able to support them in Upilio makes the results reported in Sect. 4 generalizable to a large class of IoT scenarios.

For our data collection, we execute two processing functions at the RPIs only: a `SensorReading` function, which reads the measurements via the local network from all sensors listed in a configuration file and a `PackageAssembly` function, which assembles sensor measurements into larger data packets to send to the Upilio cloud backend. Both are triggered periodically by an auxiliary timer task also implemented as a Lambda function.

The *TimerTask* implementation initializes the reading of the sensors, whereby sensor-specific data such as IP address, device ID, register address, and resource type are specified in a YAML [32] enabling Upilio to read different resources at different time intervals. *SensorReading* is a generic component that is specialized for the specific sensor type to acquire its data values. Finally, the *PackageAssembly* potentially aggregates multiple sensor readings before sending them to the backend allowing for tradeoffs between the number of data transmissions and freshness. In the case of network problems, the packets that are not confirmed from the backend are persisted locally and sent again when the connection is re-established.

3.2 Data Ingress APIs

Upilio provides two APIs for ingesting data into the system: the real-time data ingress consisting of data collector computers at the edge (the RPIs in our current setup), which transmit sensor data to Upilio as the measurements are being produced. A second interface consists of a simple file drop mechanism, which allows for the upload of current and historical data. This second mechanism is helpful for two purposes. First, it allows for the integration of data collected before real-time instrumentation as well as for backfilling data that was not transmitted in real-time, e.g., due to more extended network connectivity issues.

Real-time Data Ingest API and Data Processing. The sensor data is sent from the RPIs to the Upilio backend, which is running in the AWS cloud. Our real-time data ingest API is built on top of the publisher-subscriber system that is part of the AWS Simple Notification Service (SNS) service [12]. For each resource type (electricity, gas, water, weather data, among others) there is a corresponding SNS topic to which data of that type is sent (published) by the RPIs running the edge sites. SQS queues [13] are configured as consumers of the messages posted. Simple Queue Service (SQS) is a managed queuing service, which can be used to decouple various components of a microservices architecture, such as those employed by Upilio. Lambda functions can be configured to be triggered by data becoming available at an SQS queue. Our primary Lambda function, SqsToDdb, which is responsible for the data ingest, is triggered by data becoming available at any of the SQS queues that correspond to the SNS topics. SqsToDdb is configured to run with 128 MB, and for the sensor data we currently process, executes on average for ca. 600 ms.

We use DynamoDB [29], a highly scalable key-value store with low write and read latencies, to store all our sensor data. For the batch write that the SqsToDdb function performs, we experience average latencies of only 7–8 ms. Due to the low latency and high scalability properties, DynamoDB, and similar key-value stores are very popular in IoT scenarios, where data volume, scalability, and latency usually make relational databases impractical choices.

3.3 Serverless Frontend

Figure 1 shows a schematic representation of the Upilio serverless frontend. The key to a serverless web-based graphical user interface without operating a permanently running server lies in the fact that AWS Simple Storage Service (S3) permits making buckets word readable and that AWS buckets are addressable via web URLs. The Upilio start page with some static content and Javascript is located under a specific S3 bucket address. That page shows a login screen and requires the user to log in to our systems. The user is authenticated using the Amazon Cognito [9] identity service, in which we create a user pool to control access to the Upilio frontend system. All accesses to frontend pages (all hosted in S3) are access-controlled using that system, which hands out an access token after successful authentication.

Once the user is logged on, they see a dashboard like the ones shown in Fig. 2. On the navigation pane on the left, the user can select an overview over all connected sites (campuses), a live data view, or the analytics dashboard (shown in Fig. 2). Alternatively, the user can update their account settings or log out. To perform Upilio operations, e.g., ask the system to display specific data and perform analytics operations, we have designed a REST-interface, which was implemented using the Chalice [6] framework and the Amazon API gateway [7]. Chalice is a collection of libraries and tools to make the development of serverless micro-architecture applications easier. The Amazon API Gateway is an AWS service that makes the operation of REST-ful web APIs possible without operating your own server.

The live data view is generated via the AppSync component. AppSync is an AWS service that provides an API compatible with the open-source GraphQL [20] query language for querying and displaying graphical data, originally developed at Facebook. Upilio uses GraphQL to query DynamoDB for the sensors' current values selected in the dashboard.

Figure 2 shows the dashboard view when the user selects the option to perform OLAP-style analytics, explained in detail in Sect. 3.4. In Fig. 2 the user has selected a slice of data from the main campus (HAW), the combined sensors of all photovoltaic production at that site (labeled 'A Gesamte Leistung PAC...') together with the global radiation, measured by the campus weather station (labeled 'Globalstrahlung'), and a time range from November 11th, 00:00 h to November 12th, 00:00 h. Since the two metrics produce values of very different magnitudes, the dashboard user also selected the option to normalize the data so that they can be displayed at the same scale. The graph very neatly illustrates that the photovoltaic installation was working as expected that day, as the electric power generated almost perfectly overlays with the global radiation, i.e., sunshine present during that day.[2]

3.4   Serverless Analytics

OLAP-style analytics in Upilio is also implemented, relying entirely on the serverless paradigm. As reported in Sect. 4, this can be done efficiently and at

---

[2] In fact, Upilio uses the difference between these two normalized values to detect anomalies in the functioning of the PV inverters. Details can be found in [22].

a low cost for Upilio's use cases. Crucial in that effort is the efficient implementation of aggregation operations since they can be costly when performed inefficiently. We chose two implementation approaches: first, we use a simple aggregation approach that computes aggregations that are likely to be requested by our system's users, namely aggregations along the time dimension aggregated in buckets of daily, monthly, and yearly intervals. Then, as a second approach, we implemented the well-known blocked-range-sum algorithm [21] by Ho et al., and evaluated the performance of both (cf. Sect. 4).

Simple Data Aggregation. For the simple data aggregation implementation, a separate DynamoDB table is created for the three aggregation levels "daily", "monthly", and "yearly", which are updated on the fly using an AWS Lambda aggregation function. This function is triggered by DynamoDB Streams [3], a DynamoDB service that provides a chronologically ordered sequence of item-level changes in each DynamoDB table. The timestamp determines each granularity level's corresponding index for each record in the stream. It serves as the primary partition key for the corresponding table. For example, the timestamp is converted into the number of days passed since the beginning of UNIX time (January 1st, 1970) for the daily aggregation table. If there already is an entry in that granularity bucket, its value is read and updated with the sum of the new sensor value and the prior sum; otherwise, the new value becomes the initial bucket value. To reduce write costs, all items from the DynamoDB stream are processed first, and then the updated sum values are written back to DynamoDB in one batched write operation.

As a more sophisticated alternative for computing aggregations that also provides a mechanism of trading of aggregation speed versus additional storage, we also implemented the Blocked Range-Sum algorithm developed by Ho et al. We evaluate its cost implications in Sect. 4.2.

4 Experience and Experimental Evaluation

In this section, we first report some general experiences we had when building and operating Upilio answering whether the serverless paradigm supports building performant and cost-effective applications in the IoT domain. Then we evaluate the cost and performance of the analytics operations.

4.1 General Observations

Confirming results by others, for instance, by Lee et al. [24], we were able to observe easy deployment and provisioning of Upilio thanks to the serverless model. We used AWS Cloud Formation templates [17] to define and deploy the components of Upilio, e.g., the DynamoDB tables, SQS queues, or Lambda functions. Cloud Formation templates are JSON files that define the AWS cloud components and their connections in a scripting language. They can be used with a command-line tool to bring up, update or turn off AWS cloud components. In

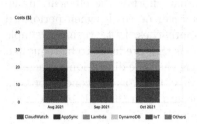

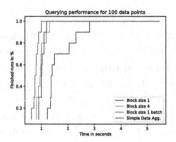

Fig. 3. The graph shows three typical months for Upilio's operational cloud computing costs. The "others" category comprises SNS, Greengrass, SQS, and S3 services.

Fig. 4. Latencies of executing queries using the pywren engine. The queries execute within an acceptable time frame, however, the pywren engine introduces some additional latency due to the launching and warmup cost for lambda functions and the data storage in S3

one experiment, we were thus able to bring up another instance of Upilio at the simple execution of a single CLI command resulting in a running instance ready for data from the edge in approximately 15 min.

4.2   Experimental Results

General Operational Costs. Besides the benefits of easier deployment of provisioning, for our university environment and its amount of data, our usual operating costs for the data acquisition storage and the (at this point) low frontend usage are on the order of 35–50$US per month. Figure 3 shows operational costs for Upilio for a typical three-month period.

First, overall cloud computing costs for the current Upilio deployment with roughy 100 sensors reporting data in minute intervals and usual analytic dashboard use is usually around forty dollars a month. Five services, Cloudwatch, AppSync, Lambda, DynamoDB, and AWS Greengrass (reported as IoT in the AWS Cost Explorer graph in Fig. 3) account for approximately 85% of the total cost, and the other services that Upilio relies on, namely SNS, SQS, and S3 combined account for only 15%. Cloudwatch [8] is AWS' service monitoring service, which we use to monitor the correct functioning of Upilio to be notified, for instance, if less than the expected number of sensor data packets arrive at the Upilio cloud API.

The AppSync costs are incurred by frontend use when users display the current live data. For the current Upilio dashboard use with a low number, i.e., approximately 10 h of usage per week, these costs are under ten dollars per month. DynamoDB costs generally vary between two and eight dollars, the variation due to different frontend usage patterns: a higher number of analysis

Table 1. Data aggregation cost for all dimensions, block size of 4.

Block Size 4				
		Cost in $ per month		
Devices	Items/Month	DynamoDB	Lambda	Total
10	432000	2.91	0.0	2.91
100	4320000	2.91	0.0	2.91
1000	43200000	49.68	0.0	49.68

Table 2. Data aggregation cost for a block size of 1 (worst case) for 100,000 dimensions.

Block Size 1				
		Cost in $ per month		
Devices	Items/Month	DynamoDB	Lambda	Total
10	432000	2.91	0.0	2.91
100	4320000	2.91	0.0	2.91
1000	43200000	18.56	0.0	18.56

operations or the use of operations resulting in more read operations will increase the DynamoDB costs.

The Upilio computation costs, i.e., operations performed by the Lambda FaaS service was approximately five dollars for the three service months in the graph. Overall, the operational costs we have found are small, particularly considering the overall functionality and the reliability of Upilio, which directly benefits from AWS' 99.99% availability of resources in a single region.

For comparison, assuming we could operate Upilio on a single server, the hardware depreciation cost alone would already be higher. With electricity and IT personnel costs, this relation tips even more in favor of a cloud-hosted serverless architecture and, almost certainly, with higher availability and reliability of the cloud-based solution.[3]

Evaluating Analytics Operations. Besides the empirically observed typical operation costs, we also evaluated the costs incurred specifically for supporting fast online analytics operations. As mentioned in Sect. 3.4, we implemented the blocked-range-sum algorithm by Ho et al. [21] in addition to the simple aggregation algorithm that aggregates daily, monthly, and yearly values to make the answering of range queries fast in the time dimension. Note that the costs for the simple aggregation algorithm are included in the graph in Fig. 3.

For our implementation of Ho et al.'s algorithm, we evaluated how the storage and Lambda computation costs changed when varying the block aggregation block size and number of sensors. In Ho's algorithm, the larger the block size, the less storage is needed for pre-aggregation at the expense of more on-the-fly costs when answering queries. Therefore, a block size of one is the worst case in terms of required storage and precomputation costs.

The cost calculations are derived from processing the data packets typically produced by our concentrator nodes, i.e., We assume that each sensor is read out once per minute and that the system is running 24/7. We assume an average length of 30 days per month to calculate the monthly costs, which leads to 43200 measurement points per sensor. We use a singular Lambda instance for data processing, which is triggered by DynamoDB Streams. The trigger is configured so that the Lambda function is only triggered with a batch size of

---

[3] Assuming a $5000 purchase cost and a five-year depreciation, the monthly cost would come to $83.

10 times the number of sensors, 1000 for our main university campus, which reads out about 100 sensors. We are considering the worst case of computing all possible aggregations, i.e., we aggregate values over 473200 possible dimensions, consisting of four (time) granularity levels, 13 units, 13 buildings, 1 domain, 7 resource types, and 100 device ids ($= 4 \times 13 \times 13 \times 1 \times 7 \times 100$). Furthermore, we make the worst-case assumption that all dimensions are updated in every batch and that all device IDs occur in every dimension. In reality, most of these aggregations would never be requested by users of our system, and as such, the cost calculations represent a worst-case scenario. While we might know a priori for some aggregations to be helpful in practice, we cannot know what the system's users will do in practice. We consider implementing one approach to start computing a particular aggregation only once requested, thereby adapting to the typical usage dynamically. Furthermore, to save space, precomputing an aggregation could be stopped again if that aggregation is not used for a certain amount of time; we plan to implement and evaluate this approach in the future.

However, even for the worst-case scenario, the monthly costs were only about $10 for the processing and persistence of the data with a block size of 1 for our university scenario. Table 2 shows the costs for a varying number of sensors and when aggregating not for all but a fixed 100,000 dimensions. When more sensors are present and more data is produced, we keep the implementation cost-efficient by making the batch size, which triggers Lambda processing, a function of the system's number of sensors. We use a linear relationship multiplying the number of sensors with 10 to set the batch size. While this choice of batch size saves computation cost, it also guarantees that the aggregations are fresh: N sensors produce N data points per minute in our environment so that aggregation data will be no more than 10 min old.

As mentioned, using a block size of one creates the worst-case for pre-aggregation storage and computation costs. Table 1 shows the costs when computing the blocked range sums using a block size of 4. The table shows that if we use a block size of 4, we could even compute and store all possible aggregations at an acceptable cost. However, even in this case, adapting the system to actual usage patterns in the frontend would also save costs, as outlined above.

Besides the monetary cost of operating Upilio, performance in terms of latency is also essential. Therefore, user queries should be executed with negligible latency. To evaluate the effectiveness of the aggregation algorithms, we performed various queries over different lengths. The experiments compare the simple data aggregation and the blocked range-sum algorithm with block sizes 1 and 4. Our experimental setup used the Pywren engine to execute multiple lambda functions that combine the appropriate aggregation values to answer user queries. The median query time was from 1 to 2 s, sufficient for our current use cases (cf. Fig. 4). However, as others have observed before, launching Lambda functions via Pywren introduces some startup latency, not least because it uses S3 buckets to store code and data. S3 has a much higher latency for data access than Dynamo DB. Therefore, as part of future work, we want to evaluate triggering the lambda functions directly from our frontend without using pywren and "keeping them warm," e.g., using a timer mechanism.

5   Conclusions

In building Upilio, we set out to examine if a scalable, cost-effective, and easily portable data collection and analysis platform for IoT sensor data can be built relying entirely on the serverless paradigm and using only off-the-shelf cloud computing building blocks. Upilio is sufficiently similar to other IoT data analytics scenarios that the results demonstrated in this paper should generalize to similar systems.

We have confirmed that developers can focus on designing and implementing functionality specific to their problem domain thanks to the flexible deployment model provided by a serverless platform like AWS Lambda. We found that the serverless paradigm enables creating scalable and performant systems without investing much time, money, or effort. Moreover, except for storage cost, which is very low, Upilio operating costs are proportionate with usage. In addition, performing operations mainly in the cloud was not a limitation for our system's data analytics use cases. Therefore, we have corroborated that creating applications using the serverless paradigm is particularly alluring for "small players" since a comprehensive system can be built with a minimal upfront cost.

In the future, we would like to perform a more detailed evaluation of the analytics operations, especially within the live system, i.e., based on typical workload demands and frontend operations.

Acknowledgements. We would like to thank the following students who have contributed to the implementation of various aspects of Upilio and its precursor: L. Brand, F. Huber, K. Kreitmeier, P. Loibl, W. Paintner, F. Saacke. P. Sacher, and L. Vögl. In addition, we thank the anonymous reviewers, whose valuable suggestions have helped us improve the final version of this paper.

References

1. Agache, A., et al.: Firecracker: lightweight virtualization for serverless applications. In: 17th USENIX Symposium on Networked Systems Design and Implementation (NSDI 2020), pp. 419–434 (2020)
2. Agarwal, A., Slee, M., Kwiatkowski, M.: Thrift: scalable cross-language services implementation. Technical report, Facebook (2007). http://thrift.apache.org/static/files/thrift-20070401.pdf
3. Amazon Web Services Inc: AWS DynamoDB Streams. https://docs.aws.amazon.com/amazondynamodb/latest/developerguide/Streams.html. Accessed 11 Sept 2019
4. Apache OpenWhisk, February 2021. https://opemwhisk.apache.org/
5. Aslanpour, M.S., et al.: Serverless edge computing: vision and challenges. In: 2021 Australasian Computer Science Week Multiconference, ACSW 2021. Association for Computing Machinery, New York (2021). https://doi.org/10.1145/3437378.3444367

6. AWS: chalice a framework for writing serverless applications, November 2020. https://aws.github.io/chalice/index
7. Amazon API Gateway, February 2021. https://aws.amazon.com/api-gateway/
8. Amazon Cloudwatch, January 2019. https://aws.amazon.com/cloudwatch/
9. Amazon Cognito, February 2021. https://aws.amazon.com/cognito/
10. Aws Greengrass, February 2021. https://aws.amazon.com/greengrass/
11. AWS Lambda, February 2021. https://aws.amazon.com/lambda/
12. AWS Simple Notification Service, February 2021. https://aws.amazon.com/sns/
13. AWS Simple Queue Service, February 2021. https://aws.amazon.com/sqs/
14. Azure Functions, February 2021. https://azure.microsoft.com/en-us/services/functions/
15. Baresi, L., Filgueira Mendonça, D., Garriga, M.: Empowering low-latency applications through a serverless edge computing architecture. In: De Paoli, F., Schulte, S., Broch Johnsen, E. (eds.) ESOCC 2017. LNCS, vol. 10465, pp. 196–210. Springer, Cham (2017). https://doi.org/10.1007/978-3-319-67262-5_15
16. Castro, P., Ishakian, V., Muthusamy, V., Slominski, A.: The rise of serverless computing. Commun. ACM 62(12), 44–54 (2019)
17. AWS Cloudformation, January 2019. https://aws.amazon.com/cloudformation/
18. Eivy, A., Weinman, J.: Be wary of the economics of "serverless" cloud computing. IEEE Cloud Comput. 4(2), 6–12 (2017). https://doi.org/10.1109/MCC.2017.32
19. Google Cloud Functions, February 2021. https://cloud.google.com/functions/
20. Graphql, November 2020. https://graphql.org/
21. Ho, C.T., Agrawal, R., Megiddo, N., Srikant, R.: Range queries in OLAP data cubes. ACM SIGMOD Rec. 26(2), 73–88 (1997)
22. Huber, F., Mock, M.: Toci: computational intelligence in an energy management system. In: 2020 IEEE Symposium Series on Computational Intelligence (SSCI). IEEE (2020)
23. IBM OpenWhisk, February 2021. https://developer.ibm.com/openwhisk/
24. Lee, H., Satyam, K., Fox, G.: Evaluation of production serverless computing environments. In: 2018 IEEE 11th International Conference on Cloud Computing (CLOUD), pp. 442–450. IEEE (2018)
25. Nastic, S., et al.: A serverless real-time data analytics platform for edge computing. IEEE Internet Comput. 21(4), 64–71 (2017)
26. Pelle, I., Czentye, J., Dóka, J., Kern, A., Gerő, B.P., Sonkoly, B.: Operating latency sensitive applications on public serverless edge cloud platforms. IEEE Internet Things J. 8(10), 7954–7972 (2021). https://doi.org/10.1109/JIOT.2020.3042428
27. Pfandzelter, T., Bermbach, D.: tinyFaaS: a lightweight FaaS platform for edge environments. In: 2020 IEEE International Conference on Fog Computing (ICFC), pp. 17–24 (2020). https://doi.org/10.1109/ICFC49376.2020.00011
28. Raspberry Pi Foundation: Raspberry Pi 4. https://www.raspberrypi.org/products/raspberry-pi-4-model-b/. Accessed 25 Aug 2019
29. Sivasubramanian, S.: Amazon dynamoDB: a seamlessly scalable non-relational database service. In: Proceedings of the 2012 ACM SIGMOD International Conference on Management of Data, pp. 729–730 (2012)
30. Sreekanti, V., et al.: Cloudburst: Stateful functions-as-a-service. Proc. VLDB Endow. 13(12), 2438–2452 (2020). https://doi.org/10.14778/3407790.3407836
31. Wang, B., Ali-Eldin, A., Shenoy, P.: Lass: running latency sensitive serverless computations at the edge. In: Proceedings of the 30th International Symposium on High-Performance Parallel and Distributed Computing, HPDC 2021, pp. 239–251. Association for Computing Machinery, New York (2021). https://doi.org/10.1145/3431379.3460646
32. YAML: YAML Ain't Markup Language, February 2021. https://yaml.org/

MAFF: Self-adaptive Memory Optimization for Serverless Functions

Tetiana Zubko, Anshul Jindal(✉) ⓘ, Mohak Chadha ⓘ, and Michael Gerndt ⓘ

Chair of Computer Architecture and Parallel Systems,
Technical University of Munich, Garching, Germany
{tetiana.zubko,anshul.jindal,mohak.chadha}@tum.de, gerndt@in.tum.de

Abstract. Function-as-a-Service (FaaS), a key enabler of serverless computing, has been proliferating, as it offers a cheap alternative for application development and deployment. However, while offering many advantages, FaaS also poses new challenges. In particular, most commercial FaaS providers still require users to manually configure the memory allocated to the FaaS functions based on their experience and knowledge. This often leads to suboptimal function performance and higher execution costs. In this paper, we present a framework called MAFF that automatically finds the optimal memory configurations for the FaaS functions based on two optimization objectives: cost-only and balanced (balance between cost and execution duration). Furthermore, MAFF self-adapts the memory configurations for the FaaS functions based on the changing function inputs or other requirements, such as an increase in the number of requests. Moreover, we propose and implement different optimization algorithms for different objectives. We demonstrate the functionality of MAFF on AWS Lambda by testing on four different categories of FaaS functions. Our results show that the suggested memory configurations with the Linear algorithm achieve 90% accuracy with a speedup of $2x$ compared to the other algorithms. Finally, we compare MAFF with two popular memory optimization tools provided by AWS, i.e., AWS Compute Optimizer and AWS Lambda Power Tuning, and demonstrate how our framework overcomes their limitations.

Keywords: serverless · cost optimization · memory optimization · duration optimization · Function-as-a-Service · memory allocation

1 Introduction

In recent years, the popularity of serverless computing technology has been proliferating in different domains [12,17,25]. Cloud users profit from the automatic scalability, faster deployments, and the possibility to outsource control and maintainability over the underlying hardware infrastructure to the cloud service providers [16,28]. Function-as-a-Service (FaaS) is a key enabler of serverless computing [29]. In FaaS, a serverless application is decomposed into simple, standalone functions uploaded to a FaaS platform such as AWS Lambda for

F. Montesi et al. (Eds.): ESOCC 2022, LNCS 13226, pp. 137–154, 2022.
https://doi.org/10.1007/978-3-031-04718-3_9

execution [28]. The pricing is charged based on the number of requests to the functions and the execution duration [9].

However, while offering many advantages, FaaS faces some challenges that hinder its widespread adoption [10,15,27]. While most infrastructure management is abstracted away from the user, major commercial FaaS providers still require users to manually configure the amount of memory allocated to the FaaS functions [26]. For most developers, this is often done by using their experience and knowledge, leading to suboptimal function performance and higher function execution costs. Furthermore, the cost of the FaaS function depends on the execution duration of the code and assigning the smallest or random memory can be considered as an anti-pattern [9,14]. Thus, the user has to do a trade-off analysis between them to define the suitable configuration for their required SLOs [21,29], and it's not trivial to find the optimal configuration where the overall cost and execution duration are both optimal.

The importance of optimizing memory configuration for the FaaS functions has already been described in various scientific works and implemented in practice [2,30]. However, the existing tools are either only implemented to be actively invoking the analyzed functions [11] or require functions to have specific settings and execution frequency to be able to provide the result [8]. To this end, we develop **MAFF** (**M**emory **A**llocation **F**ramework for **F**aaS functions), a python-based framework for automatically finding the optimal memory configurations for the FaaS functions. It is implemented in two execution modes – *active* and *passive*, depending on the way of how the function execution information is received. Our key contributions are as follows:

- We develop and present a framework called **MAFF** that automatically finds the optimal memory configurations for the FaaS functions (Sect. 3). Furthermore, it automatically self-adapts the memory configurations for the FaaS functions based on a change in the function input or other user requirements.
- We propose and implement three optimization algorithms – *Linear*, *Binary*, and *Gradient Descent*, for the minimum cost optimization objective, and two optimization algorithms – *Optimization value*, and *Duration Change*, for the balanced (balance between cost and execution duration) objective (Sect. 2).
- Although our approach is generic and *MAFF* can be easily extended to support other commercial and open-source FaaS platforms, we demonstrate the functionality of *MAFF* with AWS Lambda (Sect. 5) on four FaaS functions.
- We compare *MAFF* with other existing memory optimization tools: AWS Lambda Power Tuning [11] and AWS Compute Optimizer [8].

2   Methodology

According to business requirements, there are different optimization objectives when using FaaS functions. For example, it is essential to ensure a quick function execution in some cases. In other, the balance between the function's execution and the cost plays a more significant role. Therefore, we have considered two optimization goals:

Algorithm 1: Linear Algorithm

Input: start_mem, step_size, threshold_count, function
Output: min_cost_mem

1 step_count = 0, dur1 = **getDuration**(function, start_mem);   `// get the duration`
2 min_cost_mem = start_mem, min_cost_dur = dur1;
3 **for** *step_count ≤ threshold_count* **do**
4   old_cost = (dur1 × start_mem);
5   new_mem = start_mem + step_size;
6   dur2 = **getDuration**(function, new_mem);
7   new_cost = (dur2 × new_mem);
8   **if** *new_cost > old_cost* **then**
9   min_cost = min_cost_mem × min_cost_dur;
10   **if** *old_cost ≤ min_cost* **then**
11   min_cost_mem = start_mem, min_cost_dur = dur1;
12   **else**
13   step_count += 1;
14   **end**
15   **end**
16   dur1 = dur2, start_mem = new_mem;
17 **end**
18 **return** min_cost_mem ;   `// return the min cost memory`

- **Cost-only**: In this case, the users' primary goal is to minimize the cost of the function execution even if the duration is not the lowest.
- **Balanced:** It finds the balance between the cost and execution duration of the function. Here the goal is to find the best possible performance for a fair cost.

In the scope of this work, we developed multiple algorithms for each of the optimization goals. In the following subsections, we describe each of the algorithms.

2.1 Cost Optimization

Linear Algorithm: The main idea behind this algorithm is to continuously increase the memory allocated to the function linearly and calculate the cost for each memory configuration until a memory sweet spot is found where the optimization goal, i.e., the cost, is minimum. The pseudocode for this algorithm is shown in the Algorithm 1.

By default, it starts at the minimum memory configuration possible in AWS - 128 MB (*min_mem*) and increases the allocated memory with a pre-defined step size of 128 MB (*step_size*). Firstly, the memory of the function is set to *min_mem* and then the execution duration of the function at that memory is determined (Line 1). We further determine the cost by multiplying the allocated memory and execution duration at min_mem, since the cost is directly proportional to them [9] (Line 4). We then continuously increase the function's memory by $step\_size$ (Line 5) and determine the new execution duration of the function at that memory, and then the cost (Lines 6–7). If the cost with the new memory configuration is smaller than the previous one, the algorithm moves to the next memory iteration (Line 16). If not (Lines 8–15), the previous memory point is a minimal cost point, and the algorithm stops. However, in such a case, the algorithm could stop in the local minima. Thus, the additional logic of overcoming the local minima was added. The algorithm does not stop execution when the first local minima is found, but continues for a few more iterations until a threshold ($threshold\_count$) is reached. The higher the value of the $threshold\_count$, the more precise result can be delivered, but at the same time, more iterations will be performed.

Furthermore, typically the cost of the Lambda function stays the same with minor fluctuations until some memory level, after which it starts increasing almost linearly [19]. Following the Pareto optimization principle, when two memory configurations have the exact cost, a memory with the bigger value is selected, as it positively affects the function's execution duration.

Binary Algorithm: This algorithm is based on the classical binary search algorithm, which operates on a sorted list of numbers by iteratively comparing the searched item to the middle element of the list and eliminating parts in which the searched element can not be found. The same principle is borrowed to create this algorithm.

For finding the optimal memory, this algorithm first calculates the execution cost at the start and the middle memory configurations from the provided memory list. The user can define the memory list; by default, it is the whole range of memory values available on AWS (from `128 MB` to `10240 MB`) [5]. Suppose the cost at the start memory configuration is lower than the middle memory configuration. In that case, the algorithm continues execution on the left part of the memory array (from start to middle), otherwise on the right part. The stopping criteria for the algorithm is when the memory at the start of the analyzed memory interval is equal to the memory in its middle, meaning that the interval consists of only one value.

Gradient Descent Algorithm: This algorithm is based on the popular Gradient Decent optimization algorithm in Machine Learning. The idea is to continue finding the minimum of a metric by choosing the direction (left or right direction) towards the minimum cost at each iteration until the minimum is reached.

In this algorithm, a random memory value from the provided memory list is selected at which the cost metric is calculated along with the cost of its left neighbor. If the cost of the neighbor is higher than the cost of the current point, the algorithm continues execution on the right side of the current point (in the direction of decreasing cost, otherwise on the left side. The minimum cost is also updated if the current cost is less than the minimum cost.

The known issue with the *Gradient Descent* algorithm is that it can get stuck in the local minimum [23]. To overcome this problem, an additional counter *step_count* was added. The counter *step_count* is updated when a local minimum is reached. It is used to control that the algorithm does not stop in the first minimum that it encounters but continues execution until a threshold *threshold_count* is reached. The neighbors of the current memory configurations are found by the addition or subtraction of the memory *step_size* from the current memory value.

2.2 Balanced Optimization

In the following paragraphs, we describe two algorithms for balanced optimization goal.

Optimization-Values-Based Algorithm: The first approach to finding such an optimal point is to transform cost and execution duration into percentage format using the maximum value of cost and duration, respectively. To avoid the exhaustive search of finding maximum values [11], it is assumed that the function has maximum execution duration at the beginning of the memory list (*mem_config_list*), i.e., 128 MB and the maximum cost at the end of the list, i.e., 10240 MB. The assumption is based on the fact that increasing the allocated resources does not negatively influence a function's performance, but make its execution faster [6,19] by having more underneath resources.

The algorithm starts analyzing memories starting from 128 MB and increases memory allocated to the function with the defined memory *step_size*. For each memory configuration, the algorithm calculates a value called *optimizationValue* shown in the Eq. 1. Memory configuration having the lowest *optimizationValue* is selected as the optimal memory spot with the balanced optimization goal. As part of Eq. 1, we introduce an additional parameter, α, by which the influence of duration and cost on the final result can be adapted. The values of the parameter can range between 0 and 1. When α is equal to 0, the algorithm goal corresponds to the cost optimization, and when the α is set to 1, it will be optimizing the duration. By default, the parameter value equals 0.5, which means that both cost and duration are equally important, and a balance between them needs to be found.

$$\textbf{optimizationValue} = \frac{\alpha \times duration}{maxDuration} + \frac{(1 - \alpha) \times cost}{maxCost} \qquad (1)$$

where α is the coefficient for adjusting the influence of optimization variable (cost or duration) on the final result, and the other variables are self-explanatory from their names. The algorithm operates similarly to the Linear Algorithm, but uses *optimizationValue* as the optimization parameter. It also contains the logic of overcoming local minimums, as explained in other algorithms.

Duration Change Algorithm: This algorithm is based on the fact that, the optimal memory spot for balanced optimization goal is a point after which any additional memory increase does not provide any significant performance improvement [13]. So, the idea of this algorithm for *balanced* optimization is to incrementally increase a function's memory configurations until there is no significant improvement in its execution duration. In other words, we need to find a vertex of a hyperbola, a point at which the logarithmic curve of the function's execution duration bends. This algorithm tries to find a memory configuration after which the duration curve has flattened, and subsequent increases in memory will not significantly improve the function's performance.

The algorithm operates similarly to the Linear algorithm. By default, the algorithm starts with memory 128 MB and compares execution duration at this point to the execution duration of the next point on the right side. The memory value of the right neighbor is equal to the current memory plus the defined memory *step_size*. If the duration of the right neighbor is decreased by more than the defined change threshold percentage (γ), the algorithm continues execution for the next iteration; otherwise, execution stops. The default value of the γ is 10%, the higher the value, the closer the memory will be selected to the hyperbola vertex.

3   MAFF Framework

In this section, we present **MAFF** (**M**emory **A**llocation **F**ramework for **F**aaS functions), a python-based framework for automatically finding the optimal memory configurations for the FaaS functions according to the defined optimization goal.

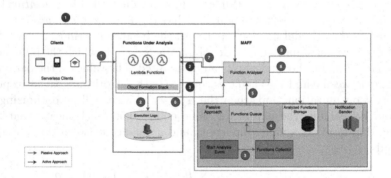

Fig. 1. High-level system architecture and workflow of *MAFF*

Figure 1 shows the high-level system architecture of *MAFF*, its components, and the workflow between them. All the components are developed in Python and deployed on AWS infrastructure. On the high level, there are two main approaches for executing *MAFF* – *active* and *passive*, differentiated by the method of how the function's execution information is gathered.

Active Approach: In the *active* approach, *MAFF* invokes function by itself. A short execution log is returned synchronously after each execution. Blue lines in Fig. 1 represent interactions between parties when using *MAFF* in the *active* approach. As can be seen, as soon as a trigger event is received by the *Functions Analyzer* (Sect. 3.1) including the optimization goal (step ❶), it performs requests to the FaaS function to find out its execution duration and cost at different memory configurations (step ❷). Then it collects execution logs and uses different algorithms described in Sect. 2 for finding the optimal configuration (step ❸). Once the configuration is found, it is then saved for the function, and *Functions Analyzer* stops its execution.

Passive Approach: In the *passive* approach, *MAFF* does not send requests to the analyzed function but relies on the real user's traffic to receive information about the function's execution. In this case, *MAFF* observes CloudWatch logs, which are generated by the Lambda function, when users invoke it. The *passive* approach of *MAFF* is developed for such scenarios, where it is not possible or not cost-efficient to actively invoke the Lambda function (e.g., if the function creates new products to the online store or adds the users to the database). When executing *MAFF* in the *passive* approach, additional components such as *Start Analysis Event, Functions Collector, Functions Queue*, are used. The flow of the passive *MAFF* approach is marked with the green lines in the Fig. 1 and starts automatically when the scheduled CloudWatch event containing optimization goal is triggered (step ❷). This event is configured to invoke the *Function Collector* Lambda function (step ❸), which gathers Amazon Resource Names (ARNs) of stack functions and adds them into an Amazon Simple Queue Service (SQS) queue (step ❹). Every new item in the queue is processed by *Functions Analyzer* Lambda for finding the optimal memory configuration at the defined optimization goal (steps ❺–❼). If *Functions Analyzer* can identify the optimal memory for the function, it adds a record into the DynamoDB database to avoid unnecessary analysis in future iterations (step ❽). *Notification Sender* sends an email notification if the memory configurations proposed by *MAFF* are significantly different from the initial configuration (step ❾).

Both *active* and *passive* approaches can adapt memory of the analyzed function in real-time on AWS Lambda as soon as the optimal memory configuration is found. Such self-adaptive configuration is performed with the help of AWS SDK for Python (Boto3). *MAFF* is a language-agnostic tool, and it can analyze any Lambda function, regardless of the programming language used for source code.

3.1   MAFF Components

Internally, *MAFF* consists of several components, each of them is based on a specific AWS service. In the following subsections, we describe its components in more detail.

Function Analyzer: This component contains the main logic of the *MAFF* and is used in both *active* and *passive* approaches. In the *active* approach, Function Analyzer sends requests to the function to generate execution logs at different memory configurations. In contrast, in the *passive* approach, it just reads all the function's logs created when users invoke the function. Further, it is responsible for analyzing those logs of the function and selecting its optimal memory configuration based on the given optimization goal and the algorithms described in Sect. 2. *Function Analyzer* itself is deployed as a Lambda function with 512 MB memory and 10 min timeout. As input, it expects the Amazon Resource Name (ARN) of the Lambda function to be analyzed.

Start Analysis Event: It is used to invoke *MAFF* in the *passive* approach. It is implemented as a scheduled AWS CloudWatch event rule, which triggers an analysis process based on the time interval specified by the user (e.g., every four hours).

Functions Collector: It is responsible for gathering ARNs of the functions which belong to a CloudFormation stack and need to be analyzed. This component is also implemented as a Lambda function with 512 MB memory and 10 min timeout. As input, this function receives the name of the CloudFormation stack.

Functions Queue: It stores the list of functions' ARNs generated by *Function Collector* before they are passed to *Function Analyzer*. It is implemented with Amazon Simple Queue Service (SQS) and uses *Function Analyzer* as a Lambda trigger.

Analyzed Functions Storage: This component stores the past optimal memory configurations of the functions found in the previous *MAFF* executions. It is implemented using the AWS DynamoDB database with function name as the primary key. This component acts as the cache, and if the function optimal memory configuration exists in the database, then the unnecessary iterations of the algorithm are avoided.

Notification Sender: It sends an email notification if the memory configurations proposed by the *MAFF* are significantly different from the initial configuration.

4   Evaluation Settings

We test the proposed *MAFF* framework for FaaS functions deployed on AWS Lambda, a popular serverless cloud platform. *MAFF* framework itself was deployed on AWS lambda as described in Sect. 3.1. Each of the algorithms introduced in Sect. 2 are executed 5 times on each of four different benchmark functions (Sect. 4.1). We also describe the evaluation scenarios conducted to evaluate *MAFF* (Sect. 4.2).

4.1   Benchmark Functions

In the evaluation, we have considered four types of functions. All of them are implemented in Python 3.8, which is one of the most popular languages used in AWS [28]. Moreover, each function was configured with a three-minute timeout, which allows them to finish execution with any memory configuration.

CPU-Intensive Function: CPU intensive functions have a logarithmic dependency between allocated memory and execution duration of the function [13]. For the test purposes of this work, a specimen CPU-bound function was created. It calculates tangent and arctangent for the numbers between 0 and 8^7.

I/O-Intensive Function: I/O function used in this work is based on a popular Linux utility for the file operations - dd [22]. Using dd, an input file /dev/zero is copied to an output file /tmp/out using 50 blocks, each of 512 bytes size. The file /dev/zero represents an unlimited flow of null characters.

Memory-Intensive Function: Memory bound function used in this work consists of a for-loop iterating from 0 to, 100000. Every iteration adds a number to the initially empty array, thus slowly filling up the memory.

Network-Intensive Function: Here a large JSON file over the Internet is read.

4.2   Evaluation Scenarios

We design our experiments to answer the following questions:

Q1. Optimal configuration finding efficiency : how efficient are the *MAFF* algorithms in finding the optimal memory configurations for various types of functions?

Q2. Optimal configuration finding accuracy: how accurate are the *MAFF* algorithms in finding the optimal memory configurations given the optimization goal?

Q3. Active vs passive approach: how do the two approaches in *MAFF* compare against each other in terms of accuracy?

5   Results

In this section, we present the results of the evaluation scenarios described in Sect. 4.2.

5.1   Q1. Optimal Configuration Finding Efficiency

Algorithms are compared based on the number of iterations and time taken by them.

Cost Optimization: Figure 2a shows the number of iterations that each of the algorithms performed to identify optimal memory configuration with the *cost optimization* as the minimization objective. For every function type, the *Linear* algorithm managed to find a minimal *cost* point with the least number of iterations. The *Binary* algorithm, in all cases, took the most steps to find a memory sweet spot. It can be explained by the fact that memory points with minimal cost for all function types lay in the region 128 MB–1280 MB. But *Binary* algorithm was executed on the whole memory range (128 MB–10240 MB), which took more steps to narrow the search to the correct memory region. For every function type, *Gradient Descent* required more steps than *Linear* algorithm and less than *Binary* algorithm to find the optimal memory spot.

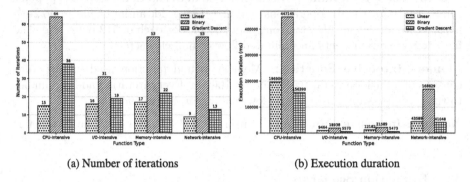

(a) Number of iterations   (b) Execution duration

Fig. 2. The required number of iterations and the execution duration of the various algorithms for the cost optimization objective.

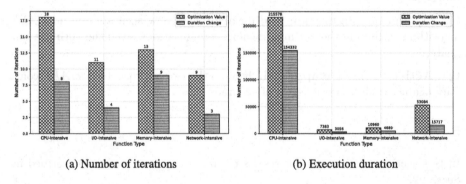

(a) Number of iterations   (b) Execution duration

Fig. 3. The number of iterations and execution duration for various algorithms for the balanced optimization objective.

Additionally, from the Fig. 2b showcasing the average execution duration of each algorithm, one can observe that the *Binary* algorithm has the highest execution duration for all function types. This also corresponds to the fact that this algorithm requires the highest number of iterations to find an optimal memory configuration. *Linear* algorithm performed better than the *Gradient Descent* in terms of the required iterations. However, *Gradient Descent* algorithm outperformed the *Linear* one in terms of the execution duration. For all the functions, *Gradient Descent* has the shortest execution duration.

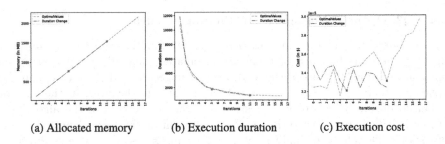

(a) Allocated memory   (b) Execution duration   (c) Execution cost

Fig. 4. Changes in different metrics with the iterations of the three algorithms for balanced optimization objective concerning the CPU benchmark.

Table 1. Memory configurations selected for the cost optimization objective.

Function Type	Optimal (in MB)	Linear (in MB)	Binary (in MB)	GD (in MB)
CPU-Intensive	<1280	845	1047	900
I/O-Intensive	<1280	794	2071	767
Memory-Intensive	<1152	947	1723	973
Network-Intensive	<256	154	130	370

Binary algorithm shows the worst results; however, it can be explained by the fact that optimal memory configuration was located closer to the beginning of the memory interval. Thus, as the interval for the algorithm execution was wide (128 MB–10240 MB), it took many iterations for the algorithm to find the optimal memory configuration.

Balanced Optimization: As it can be seen from Fig. 3a, in general *Duration Change* algorithm requires fewer iterations to find the optimal memory configuration compared to the *Optimization Value* algorithm. The *Duration Change* algorithm uses the definition proposed by AWS, which says that the balance between cost and duration is achieved at the memory, at which the duration curve of the function bends [13]. In the *Optimization Value* algorithm, it is assumed that the balance point of the function is such at which minimal duration can be achieved for the smallest cost, following Eq. 1. This algorithm usually selects the higher memory values (on the right side of the duration curve's knee). From Fig. 3b, showing the average execution duration of both algorithms, one can observe that, for all function types, the *Optimization Value* algorithm required more time than the *Duration Change* algorithm, which is proportional to the number of iterations required by them.

Furthermore, Fig. 4 shows how different parameters (cost, execution duration, and cost) behave for the CPU benchmark function when executed for the two algorithms with the balanced optimization objective. The resulting optimal configuration for each case is highlighted in all the three sub-figures.

5.2   Q2. Optimal Configuration Finding Accuracy

As the duration and cost profiles of every test function are known, optimal memory intervals for each of them are calculated manually (displayed under optimal in Table 1). Thus, if the algorithm managed to find the memory in the optimal interval, its result is assumed to be correct. However, in the case of balanced optimization objective, estimating the correctness of the algorithms is more challenging as there is no clear definition of the term "optimal memory spot". Therefore, we only show accuracy measures for cost and duration optimization objectives in the below paragraphs.

Cost Optimization: To evaluate the correctness of algorithms, the average result of their five executions for every benchmark function was calculated and compared to the correct memory intervals. Due to the variability of a cloud environment and lack of user control over it, it is hard to predict the exact memory configurations with which function will be executed with the lowest cost. Thus, based on the data received from the function's profiles (Sect. 4.1), optimal memory interval is defined as an interval in which the optimal memory spot can be located. The second column in Table 1 specifies the optimal memory interval for every function type. The next columns show average memory levels selected by each algorithm. If the selected memory level by the algorithm is inside the correct interval, we consider its result to be correct, and the corresponding table cell is marked green. Otherwise, the result is wrong and marked red.

For all function types, the *Linear* algorithm output results in the correct memory interval. *Binary* and *Gradient Descent* algorithms managed to find optimal memory configurations for two and three functions, respectively. To better evaluate the accuracy of the algorithms for the cost optimization objective, we conducted an experiment where each algorithm was executed five times for each of the four example functions, so there are twenty executions in total. The experiment concluded that, *Linear* algorithm has the highest accuracy - 95%, *Gradient Descent* - 85%, and *Binary* - 55%.

5.3   Q3. Active vs Passive Approach

As part of this evaluation, we only discuss the results of the balanced optimization goal deployed with the *Duration Change* algorithm. Figure 5 shows the scheme of execution *MAFF* in the *passive* approach used as part of this work for evaluation. Four test functions (CPU-, I/O-, memory- and network-intensive) were deployed in one CloudFormation stack and invoked every 5 min by a scheduled CloudWatch Event (Event A). This event was used to simulate user invocations. After each execution, corresponding log data was generated and stored in the CloudWatch service. In parallel to that, the analysis process for finding optimal memory configuration was also executed. The process was triggered by another CloudWatch scheduled event (Event B) with 30 min intervals. Thus, there were six function executions between every analysis round. Event B was configured to invoke the Function Collector Lambda function, which gathered ARNs of stack functions and added them into the SQS queue. Every new item in the queue was processed by Analyzer Lambda, which evaluated execution logs of the corresponding function. If Analyzer could identify the optimal memory for the function, it added a record into the DynamoDB database to avoid unnecessary analysis in future iterations. The whole experiment lasted for 6 h, during which every of the test functions was executed 72 times and the analyzer function 12 times. It was enough to find optimal memories for all functions in the stack. As expected (Table 2), memory values selected by both approaches are quite similar, with some minor differences due to fluctuations in the value of the function's execution duration.

6   Comparison to Analogs

In this section, *MAFF* was compared to two popular resource optimization tools: AWS Compute Optimizer (ACO) [8] and AWS Lambda Power Tuning (ALPT) [11]. All experiments were performed on CPU-intensive function and the optimization objective was set to *cost* for *MAFF* and ALPT. *MAFF* was configured to use *Linear* algorithm for *active* and *passive* approaches. Optimization goal cannot be selected for ACO.

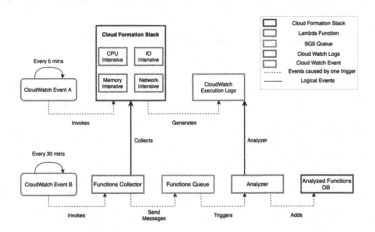

Fig. 5. Scheme of experiment on MAFF in passive approach.

Table 2 shows a comparison between *MAFF* in *active* and *passive* approaches to its two analogs. Optimal memory suggested by the tools is quite different, but for both MAFF approaches and ALPT, the resulting value lies in the correct memory interval defined in Sect. 4.1. Memory suggested by ACO is below the defined interval (initial memory was set to 128 MB). ACO has the most strict requirements for its execution than all other tools. There must be at least 50 function invocations in the last 14 d, and memory allocated to the function must not be higher than 1792 MB [8]. For *MAFF* in the *passive* approach, the algorithm should have enough log values to perform analysis, and the number can vary depending on the function.

Execution duration for *MAFF* (*active* approach) and ALPT are similar - around 3 min per analysis. ACO can take up to 12 h to find an optimal memory value. *MAFF* (*passive* approach) requires only 12 s for execution, on the condition that enough log values are provided. ALPT uses exhaustive search to identify optimal memory level for a cost, or execution duration. By default, this tool will need to perform at least 225 requests to the function to identify the optimal memory point. AWS Compute Optimizer is provided free of charge, while other optimization tools incur additional costs. The cost per analysis provided in this table can vary depending on the analyzed function and amount of steps the algorithm needs to perform, but in general, *MAFF* in both approaches is cost-efficient than the others.

While performing experiments on AWS Compute Optimizer, an interesting behavior of the tool was observed. To demonstrate it, a CPU-intensive function was deployed on four separate Lambda instances in eu-central-1 AWS region. Each of the functions was allocated different memories: 128 MB, 256 MB, 512 MB, and 1024 MB invoked every 5 min by the scheduled CloudWatch Event [7]. It was expected that the tool would suggest one optimal memory for the CPU-

Table 2. Comparison of *MAFF* to its analogs

	M–Active	M–Passive	ACO	ALPT
Suggested Memory	845	896	160	1024
Requirements	None	Approx. 20 function's invocations	Minimum 50 invocations, less than 1792 MB allocated	None
Duration of Analysis	3 min 16 s	11 s	up to 12 h	2 min 30 s
Cost	0.0025	0.0012	0	0.0131
Automatic Value Setup	Yes	Yes	No	Yes

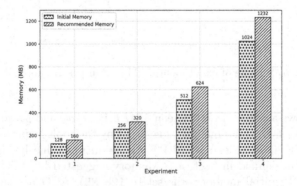

Fig. 6. Experiment on AWS compute optimizer showcasing wrong optimal memory suggested for the same function allocated with different initial memory configurations.

intensive function regardless of the initial memory level with which the function was created, as the application logic and workload for all functions is the same. However, after 12 h of the experiment, AWS Compute Optimizer suggested different memories for each of the functions. Figure 6 shows the memory values proposed by Compute Optimizer for each function. For all of them, the tool recommended increasing memory value. Thus, the tool does not suggest the optimal memory configurations but relies on the initial memory allocated and increases them always.

7 Related Work

With the advent of serverless computing, there is a significant amount of research aimed at optimizing cloud computing resource utilization [2,3,11,20]. There has been some work on the performance profiling of various FaaS platforms. Wang et al. [28] performed an in-depth study of resource management and performance isolation with three popular serverless computing providers: AWS Lambda, Azure Functions, and Google Cloud Functions. Their analysis demonstrates a reasonable difference in performance between the FaaS platforms. Furthermore, Shahrad et al. [24] studied the architectural implications of serverless computing and pointed out that the short function runtimes hamper exploitation of system architectural features like temporal locality and reuse in FaaS. Chadha et al. [13] examine the underlying processor architectures for Google Cloud Functions (GCF) and determine the optimization of FaaS functions using Numba can improve performance by and save costs on average.

Furthermore, a significant number of research works aim to optimize the memory and cost for the FaaS functions. COSE [2] framework finds the optimal configurations for a FaaS function using the Bayesian Optimization algorithm while minimizing the total cost of execution. It models the behavior of a function and the environment (cloud, edge) in which those functions are deployed. However, they optimized based on cost only, does not guarantee the accuracy of the process, and can only be used in active mode. Bayesian Optimization was also used in CherryPick [4] tool for creating performance models for different cloud applications. The system provides 45-90% accuracy in finding optimal configurations and decreases cost up to 25%. But, they focused on traditional cloud applications. Another framework, Astra [18], is designed to optimize FaaS function configurations for specifically map-reduce usecase.

Google has developed a recommendation system to help the users choose the optimal virtual machine (VM) type [1]. It currently does not support Google Cloud Functions. As discussed in Sect. 6, AWS Compute Optimizer [8] can only be executed for the functions whose allocated memory level is less or equal to 1792 MB and invoked at least 50 times in the last two weeks. AWS Lambda Power Tuning [11] tool uses exhaustive search to identify optimal memory level for a cost or execution duration. AWS Lambda Power Tuning is quite similar to MAFF in terms of lack of requirements, quick analysis time, and the possibility to set up recommended memory automatically. But users can use the AWS

Lambda Power Tuning tool only in active mode, which can be impossible or not recommended for some business scenarios. Thus, the MAFF tool developed in this work outperforms AWS Compute Optimizer in the time required for the analysis, and provides a possibility to execute the tool in the *passive* approach.

None of the aforementioned research efforts address the issue of automatically configuring the optimal memory of FaaS functions from different objectives. The proposed tool *MAFF* fills that gap.

8   Conclusion

Serverless computing has abstracted most cloud server management decisions away from the users but configuring the memory of FaaS functions: a low-level configuration, which directly influences the performance and cost of the FaaS functions, is still left up to the users. To solve this problem, we introduced **MAFF**[1] to find optimal memory configuration for the FaaS function based on two optimization objectives: *cost*, and *balanced* (Sect. 2). For cost objective, it was possible to achieve 90% of accuracy using the *Linear* algorithm with at least two times smaller number of steps as compared to others. For achieving the *balanced* optimization goal, *Optimization Value* and *Duration Change* algorithms were used. We further introduced two different approaches for performing memory optimization - *active* and *passive*, differs based on the method of collecting the functions execution logs (Sect. 3). We also showcase *MAFF* advantages over the others in terms of cost and finding the optimal memory configurations (Sect. 6).

In the future, we plan to extend *MAFF* with other public serverless compute providers. Adding the functionality of tracking updates in the program code of the analyzed function is another prospect.

Acknowledgements. This work was supported by the funding of the German Federal Ministry of Education and Research (BMBF) in the scope of the Software Campus program. The authors also thank the anonymous reviewers whose comments helped in improving this paper.

References

1. Google cloud recommendations (2018). https://cloud.google.com/compute/docs/instances/apply-machine-type-recommendations-for-instances. Accessed 17 June 2021
2. Akhtar, N., Raza, A., Ishakian, V., Matta, I.: COSE: configuring serverless functions using statistical learning. In: IEEE INFOCOM 2020 - IEEE Conference on Computer Communications, pp. 129–138 (2020). https://doi.org/10.1109/INFOCOM41043.2020.9155363
3. Akin, M.: How does proportional CPU allocation work with AWS Lambda? Opsgenie Engineering. https://engineering.opsgenie.com/how-does-proportional-cpu-allocation-work-with-aws-lambda-41cd44da3cac

---

[1] https://github.com/tetzubko/self-adaptive-memory-faas.

4. Alipourfard, O., Liu, H.H., Chen, J., Venkataraman, S., Yu, M., Zhang, M.: CherryPick: adaptively unearthing the best cloud configurations for big data analytics. In: Proceedings of the 14th USENIX Conference on Networked Systems Design and Implementation, NSDI 2017, pp. 469–482. USENIX Association (2017)
5. AWS: AWS Lambda - Serverless Compute. https://aws.amazon.com/lambda/
6. AWS: Choosing the Optimal Memory Size - Serverless Architectures with AWS Lambda. https://docs.aws.amazon.com/whitepapers/latest/serverless-architectures-lambda/choosing-the-optimal-memory-size.html
7. AWS: Creating a CloudWatch Events Rule That Triggers on a Schedule - Amazon CloudWatch Events. https://docs.aws.amazon.com/AmazonCloudWatch/latest/events/Create-CloudWatch-Events-Scheduled-Rule.html
8. AWS: Supported resources and requirements - AWS Compute Optimizer. https://docs.aws.amazon.com/compute-optimizer/latest/ug/requirements.html#requirements-lambda-functions
9. AWS: Aws lambda pricing (2020). https://aws.amazon.com/lambda/pricing/
10. Baldini, I., et al.: Serverless computing: current trends and open problems. In: Chaudhary, S., Somani, G., Buyya, R. (eds.) Research Advances in Cloud Computing, pp. 1–20. Springer, Singapore (2017). https://doi.org/10.1007/978-981-10-5026-8_1
11. Casalboni, A.: AWS Lambda Power Tuning. https://github.com/alexcasalboni/aws-lambda-power-tuning
12. Chadha, M., Jindal, A., Gerndt, M.: Towards federated learning using FaaS fabric. In: Proceedings of the 2020 Sixth International Workshop on Serverless Computing, WoSC 2020, pp. 49–54. Association for Computing Machinery, New York (2020). https://doi.org/10.1145/3429880.3430100
13. Chadha, M., Jindal, A., Gerndt, M.: Architecture-specific performance optimization of compute-intensive FaaS functions. In: 2021 IEEE 14th International Conference on Cloud Computing (CLOUD), pp. 478–483 (2021). https://doi.org/10.1109/CLOUD53861.2021.00062
14. Eismann, S., Bui, L., Grohmann, J., Abad, C., Herbst, N., Kounev, S.: Sizeless: predicting the optimal size of serverless functions, pp. 248–259. Association for Computing Machinery, New York (2021). https://doi.org/10.1145/3464298.3493398
15. Eivy, A.: Be wary of the economics of "serverless" cloud computing. IEEE Cloud Comput. 4(2), 6–12 (2017). https://doi.org/10.1109/MCC.2017.32
16. Fan., C., Jindal., A., Gerndt., M.: Microservices vs serverless: a performance comparison on a cloud-native web application. In: Proceedings of the 10th International Conference on Cloud Computing and Services Science - CLOSER, pp. 204–215. INSTICC, SciTePress (2020). https://doi.org/10.5220/0009792702040215
17. Grafberger, A., Chadha, M., Jindal, A., Gu, J., Gerndt, M.: FedLess: secure and scalable federated learning using serverless computing. In: 2021 IEEE International Conference on Big Data (Big Data), pp. 164–173, December 2021. https://doi.org/10.1109/BigData52589.2021.9672067
18. Jarachanthan, J., Chen, L., Xu, F., Li, B.: Astra: autonomous serverless analytics with cost-efficiency and QoS-awareness. In: 2021 IEEE International Parallel and Distributed Processing Symposium (IPDPS), pp. 756–765 (2021). https://doi.org/10.1109/IPDPS49936.2021.00085
19. Jindal, A., Chadha, M., Benedict, S., Gerndt, M.: Estimating the capacities of function-as-a-service functions. In: Proceedings of the 14th IEEE/ACM International Conference on Utility and Cloud Computing Companion, UCC 2021 Companion. Association for Computing Machinery, New York (2021). https://doi.org/10.1145/3492323.3495628

20. Jindal, A., Frielinghaus, J., Chadha, M., Gerndt, M.: Courier: delivering serverless functions within heterogeneous FaaS deployments. In: Proceedings of the 14th IEEE/ACM International Conference on Utility and Cloud Computing, UCC 2021. Association for Computing Machinery, New York (2021). https://doi.org/10.1145/3468737.3494097

21. Jindal, A., Gerndt, M.: From DevOps to NoOps: is it worth it? In: Ferguson, D., Pahl, C., Helfert, M. (eds.) Cloud Computing and Services Science, pp. 178–202. Springer International Publishing, Cham (2021)

22. Linux: dd(1) - Linux manual. https://man7.org/linux/man-pages/man1/dd.1.html

23. Ruder, S.: An overview of gradient descent optimization algorithms. Technical report (2017). http://caffe.berkeleyvision.org/tutorial/solver.html

24. Shahrad, M., Balkind, J., Wentzlaff, D.: Architectural implications of function-as-a-service computing. In: Proceedings of the 52nd Annual IEEE/ACM International Symposium on Microarchitecture, pp. 1063–1075 (2019)

25. Shankar, V., et al.: Serverless linear algebra. In: Proceedings of the 11th ACM Symposium on Cloud Computing, SoCC 2020, pp. 281–295. Association for Computing Machinery, New York (2020). https://doi.org/10.1145/3419111.3421287

26. Spillner, J.: Resource management for cloud functions with memory tracing, profiling and autotuning. In: WOSC 2020 - Proceedings of the 2020 6th International Workshop on Serverless Computing, Part of Middleware 2020, pp. 13–18. Association for Computing Machinery Inc., New York, December 2020. https://doi.org/10.1145/3429880.3430094

27. Steinbach, M., Jindal, A., Chadha, M., Gerndt, M., Benedict, S.: TppFaas: modeling serverless functions invocations via temporal point processes. IEEE Access **10**, 9059–9084 (2022). https://doi.org/10.1109/ACCESS.2022.3144078

28. Wang, L., Li, M., Zhang, Y., Ristenpart, T., Swift, M.: Peeking behind the curtains of serverless platforms. In: 2018 USENIX Annual Technical Conference (USENIX ATC 18), pp. 133–146. USENIX Association (2018)

29. Serverless Working Group: CNCF WG-serverless whitepaper v1. 0, March 2018. https://gw.alipayobjects.com/os/basement_prod/24ec4498-71d4-4a60-b785-fa530456c65b.pdf. Accessed 15 July 2020

30. Zhang, M., Zhu, Y., Zhang, C., Liu, J.: Video processing with serverless computing: a measurement study (2019). https://doi.org/10.1145/3304112.3325608

Author Index

Printed in the United States
by Baker & Taylor Publisher Services